TIBET'S HIDDEN WILDERNESS

TIBET'S HIDDEN

Wildlife and Nomads of
the Chang Tang Reserve

WILDERNESS

Text and Photographs by George B. Schaller

Harry N. Abrams, Inc., Publishers

EDITOR: Sharon AvRutick
DESIGNER: Dana Sloan
PHOTO EDITOR: John K. Crowley

Library of Congress Cataloging-in-Publication Data
Schaller, George B.
    Tibet's hidden wilderness: wildlife and nomads of the Chang
Tang Reserve/text and photographs by George B. Schaller.
            p.   cm.
    Includes bibliographical references (p.   ) and index.
    ISBN 0–8109–3893–6 (clothbound)
    1. Zoology—China—Chang Tang Reserve—Anecdotes.
    2. Nomads—China—Chang Tang Reserve—Anecdotes.
    3. Chang Tang Reserve (China)—Anecdotes. 4. Schaller,
    George B. I. Title.
QL307.S33   1997
508.51'5—dc21   97–821

Printed and bound in Japan

Harry N. Abrams, Inc.
100 Fifth Avenue
New York, N.Y. 10011
www.abramsbooks.com

Pages 2–3: Like figures in a Chinese screen painting, chiru drift
across a snow-covered plain. The herd includes adult males, year-
ling males with short horns, females, and young.

Map by Christine Edwards

Excerpt from "Vulture" (page 50):
From SELECTED POEMS by Robinson Jeffers.
Copyright © 1963 by Garth Jeffers and Donnan Jeffers.
Reprinted by permission of Random House, Inc.

The author would like to express his deepest gratitude to
Sharon AvRutick, Dana Sloan, and John Crowley for their
excellent editing and design, as well as their care in bringing
this book to publication.

Contents

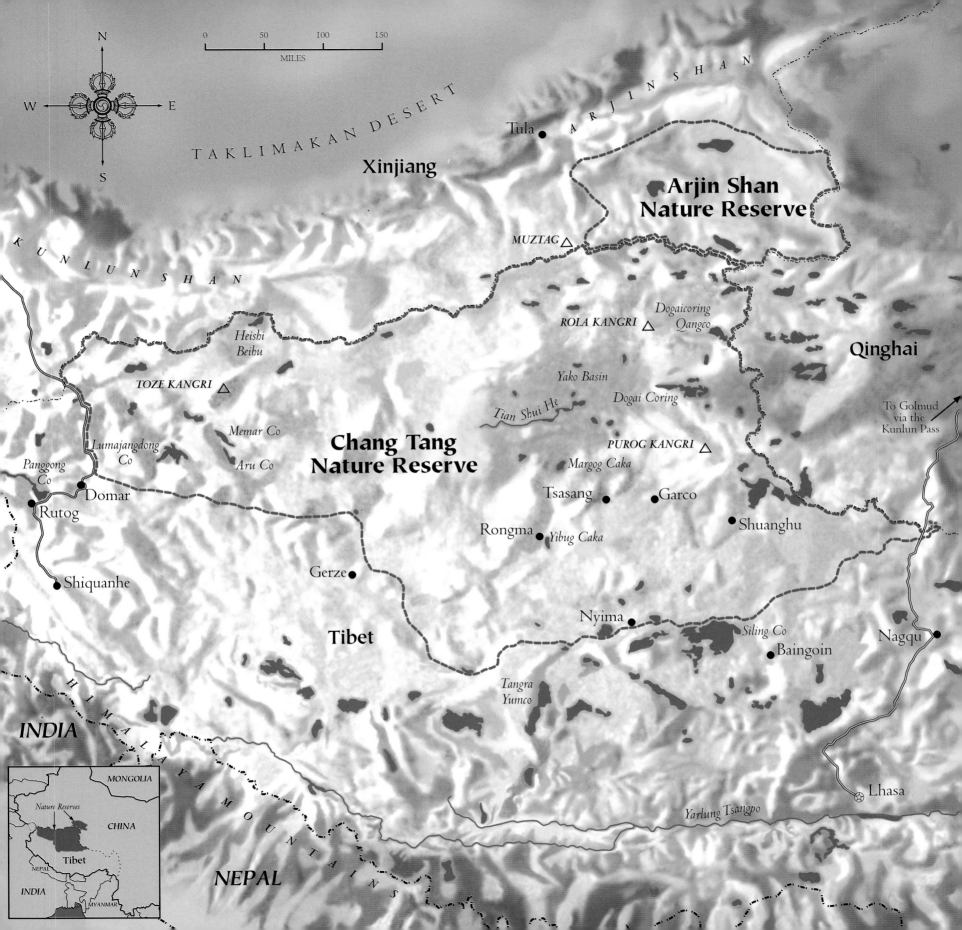

N

W ⟷ E

S

TAKLIMAKAN DESERT

Xinjiang

Tula

ARJIN SHAN

**Arjin Shan
Nature Reserve**

MUZTAG △

KUNLUN SHAN

*Heishi
Beihu*

ROLA KANGRI △

*Dogaicoring
Qangco*

Qinghai

TOZE KANGRI △

Yako Basin

Dogai Coring

Tian Shui He

Memar Co

**Chang Tang
Nature Reserve**

PUROG KANGRI △

To Golmud
via the
Kunlun Pass

*Lumajangdong
Co*

Aru Co

Margog Caka

*Panggong
Co*

Tsasang

Garco

Domar

Rongma

Yibug Caka

Shuanghu

Rutog

Gerze

Shiquanhe

Nyima

Tibet

Siling Co

Baingoin

Nagqu

*Tangra
Yumco*

HIMALAYA MOUNTAINS

INDIA

NEPAL

Lhasa

Yarlung Tsangpo

MONGOLIA

Nature Reserves

CHINA

Tibet

NEPAL

Tibet

INDIA

MYANMAR

0   50   100   150

MILES

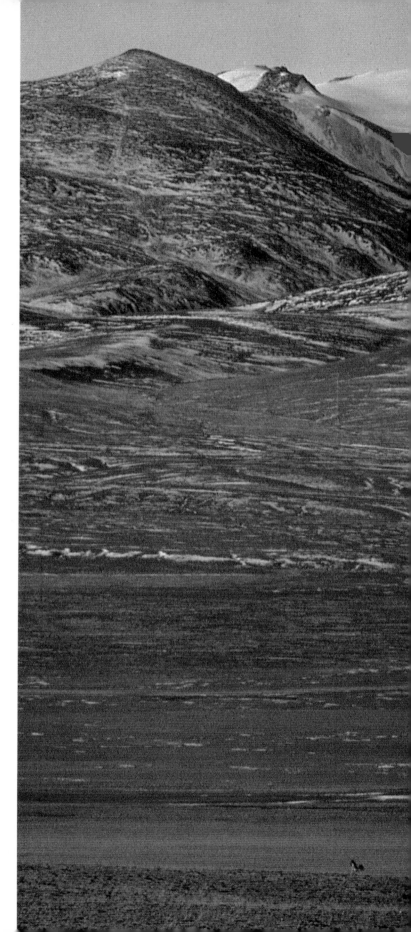

ABOVE: Two kiang in the Aru Basin.
RIGHT: A kiang herd gallops across the winter steppe.

According to Tibetan legend, somewhere in northern Tibet, ringed by mountains and hidden in mist and cloud, is the kingdom of Shambala where hunger, poverty, and illness are unknown and people live for more than a century. There, our sacred knowledge and the source of our spirit are kept in a shining palace in the city of Kalapa. Someday, when nations have exhausted themselves through war, greed, and ignorance, the king of Shambala will ride into the world, destroy the forces of evil, and bring forth a new golden age that will persist for a millennium.

The search for a mystical Shambala is a journey of the heart, a metaphorical search for harmony, and a solution to the riddle of our existence. I did not find the city of Kalapa in the Chang Tang.

ABOVE: The southeastern part of the Chang Tang receives more precipitation than the rest, as much as twelve inches a year, enough to form lush alpine meadows on mountain slopes.

OPPOSITE: A summer snowstorm lashes distant hills. Most of the annual precipitation falls between late June and September, leaving winter skies clear and cold.

This center of heaven,
This core of the earth,
This heart of the world,
Fenced round with snow,
The headland of all rivers,
Where the mountains are high and
The land is pure.

Tibetan poem, 8th–9th century

ABOVE: A chiru male, resplendent in full nuptial pelage, courts a female by remaining close to her and trying to prevent her from leaving his vicinity.

RIGHT: On their southward trek in early August, almost invisible against the mountains, chiru females and young migrate toward a pass in the crystal peaks of the Aru Range.

Preface

The road climbs up through a gaunt canyon in China's Qinghai Province. Near the crest the sky expands, and the hills become round, dazzling white after a heavy snowfall. We halt briefly on the 15,700-foot Kunlun Pass, then continue into the Chang Tang, its hills and plains a blinding expanse rolling southward to the edge of vision. I ask our driver to stop. Resting my scope on the car's hood, I scan the terrain while my Chinese coworkers wait. It is deadly still, and the white plains seem lifeless, cut by the dark thread of road continuing to Lhasa. But on a far slope I spot Tibetan wild asses, or kiang, as the Tibetans call them, and with one sweep of the scope I count 262 standing alone or in clusters. Beyond are several small herds of Tibetan antelope, or chiru, the animals pawing through snow in search of forage. Although cold stabs through my down jacket and my fingers are numb on the scope, I am elated. For the first time, on this October day in 1985, I behold the Chang Tang, even if only its eastern edge. Finally, my imagination meets reality, a wild and bleak land where humankind has barely intruded and animals live as if becalmed in time and space.

Chang Tang is Tibetan for Northern Plain. But words have feeling as well as meaning. Chang Tang is a powerful, seductive name that conveys vast empty spaces and howling skies. Here was a landscape out of my past, one I had made my own when, as a boy, I dreamed through Sven Hedin's books, reveling in descriptions such as this: "We penetrated deeper and deeper into the unknown, putting one mountain chain after the other behind us. And from every pass a new landscape unfolded its wild, desolate vistas towards a new and mysterious horizon." Sven Hedin, the great Swedish explorer, made three long expeditions through this area, the most remote part of the Tibetan Plateau, his final trip lasting from 1906 to 1908.

Lying in the shadow of the Himalaya at elevations below thirteen thousand feet, southern and eastern Tibet have a benign climate with forests and fields, towns and monasteries. But there is another Tibet, much of it above fifteen thousand feet, with treeless steppes and windswept ranges where only nomadic pastoralists with their herds of yaks, sheep, and goats can exist, and where there are vast tracts so barren that even they cannot survive. This is the Chang Tang. From the southeast corner of Qinghai the Chang Tang extends west across Tibet and north into Xinjiang toward the Kunlun and Arjin mountains.

The Tibetan Plateau, 950,000 square miles in size, fenced in by the Himalaya, Karakoram, Kunlun, Arjin, and other imposing ranges, had its origin about forty to fifty million years ago when, drifting northward, the Indian subcontinent smashed into the southern edge of Asia. India's northern edge slid a short distance under Asia's rim, buckling the crust to form the Himalaya. Compression and thrust-faulting led to the raising of the plateau. After a period of quiescence, the plateau uplifted again twenty million years ago, and yet again in a final major upheaval eight million years ago during the late Miocene to create today's topography. Only the eastern and southern parts have outlets to the ocean, with such rivers as the Yellow, Yangtze, Mekong, and Yarlung Tsangpo (which downstream becomes the Brahmaputra). Much of the remaining plateau, including the Chang Tang, consists of lake basins surrounded by hills. Some basins are dry, and others have lakes devoid of outlets with water that is saline or brackish; only a few glacier-fed lakes have drinkable water. Ranges and isolated massifs with ice-capped peaks, at times over twenty thousand feet high, rise in hard grandeur above the expanse of hill and plain, steppe and desert.

My heart lay in the northern part of the Chang Tang, the most desolate region of this Miocene landscape, where nomads were few and where such animals as wild yaks, chiru, kiang, Tibetan argali sheep, Tibetan gazelles, and Tibetan brown bears—all unique to the Tibetan Plateau—lured me. The more distant and elusive a species, the greater the challenge to chronicle its life. I like to explore in the physical as well as the intellectual realm, and over the years have sought, among others, snow leopards in the Himalaya of Pakistan and Nepal, jaguars in the swamps of Brazil's Mato Grosso, giant pandas in China's bamboo forests, wild camels in the Gobi Desert of Mongolia, and mountain gorillas in the rainforests of Zaire. But always there remained the Chang Tang of my boyhood. Is it possible to be homesick for a world unknown?

I grew up at a time when Tibet was still a place of longing, fantasy, and escape; a place of spiritual purity and wisdom. It was a land of mystery, its isolating immensity barely explored by the Western world. Tibet had been intermittently allied to China in a complex relationship for centuries, until in 1911, with the collapse of the Qing Dynasty, it in effect became independent, with its own money, army, and foreign service. All Chinese were expelled. The Western expeditions that had so persistently attempted to reach the holy city of Lhasa, the cultural and spiritual heart of Tibet, ceased as borders were closed by the Tibetan army. Toward the end of the 1800s, Tibet had become a pawn in the struggle for power between England and Russia. Now it preferred to stay aloof from the world and rigidly withdrew into itself.

But the international community did not officially recognize Tibet's independence, and China did not relinquish its perceived suzerainty. In October 1950 China invaded and routed Tibet's army. This led to an agreement that acknowledged China's sovereignty but gave Tibet the right to maintain its traditional political and religious systems. Relations between China and Tibet deteriorated and culminated in a Tibetan uprising during March 1959. It was quashed, the Dalai Lama fled into exile, and with China now in complete control, Tibet's old society was at an end.

The Tibetan Plateau remained sealed to outsiders, but I retained my longing. I did not seek to fill blanks on the map, or probe some aspect of Tibetan Buddhism, or live a romantic myth; I sought to study and, if needed, help conserve a unique wildlife community.

Tensions within China relaxed in the late 1970s and from 1980 onward the Tibet Autonomous Region permitted some tourism, encouraged economic development, and eased many other restrictions. When I first visited Lhasa in 1980, I immediately felt the symbolic and sacred aura of the town. The Dalai Lama had left but his spirit remained. The Potala, his former home, magical in its serenity and beauty, still grows seamlessly from its mountain, a shining galleon, white and ochre with golden roofs, afloat among heaving peaks as if in a phantom sea. And the Jokhang, the holiest of temples, remains as a sacred sanctuary that the faithful circumambulate after long journeys from all parts of the Tibetan Plateau.

My quest for the Chang Tang obviously contained elements of a mystical pursuit of the past, but even my first weeks there in 1985 made me aware of today's reality. I had learned that the wildlife of the Chang Tang did indeed need someone to speak on its behalf. All too often conservation efforts are made in response to crises, after wildlife has been decimated and habitat destroyed, or after species have been irretrievably lost and become mere shadows of memory. The Chang Tang provided a rare opportunity to study, protect, and manage an entire undamaged ecosystem.

In that same October of 1985, a blizzard had covered the Chang Tang with a foot of snow, a rare event. Usually winds and sun quickly expose patches of ground after a snowfall, but this time it was calm and crushingly cold. Chiru migrated far out of their usual winter range in search of forage, plowing knee-deep through snow. Soon thousands were starving, and in the great white silence they reclined, never to rise, while snow drifted against their bodies. To find forage, kiang pawed craters in crusted snow until their lower legs were raw. Truck drivers shot animals that strayed near the road to sell the meat in towns.

On a tractor-pulled wagon we traveled cross-country for nine days to check on

LEFT: A chiru male paws a crater in the snow to reach the scant forage. In winter plants are dead or senescent and low in nutrients. An animal may expend more energy in obtaining food than it receives in return, and, if snow persists, it may quickly die of malnutrition.

BELOW: Kiang were also affected by the October 1985 blizzard. But being larger than chiru, they expended proportionately less energy in digging for forage, and few died.

PRECEDING PAGES: The Chang Tang consists of many basins, some dry and others with lakes, surrounded by desolate hills and ranges. About a quarter of the reserve consists of mountains with little or no vegetation, and some fifty peaks reach twenty thousand feet or higher.

wildlife and on the nomads. Miles apart, isolated by an infinity of white, were clusters of two to three black tents of woven yak hair. Dejected-looking sheep clustered by the tents near the raw carcasses and flayed hides of their starved relatives. Beside one tent was a carnage of wildlife—seven blue sheep, five kiang, one chiru, and one gazelle—hunting of the weakened animals obviously easy. At each encampment we were invited inside with typical Tibetan hospitality and offered cups of salted and buttered tea, as we sat to the right of the central fire as custom demanded. A woman would pump a goat-skin bellows with her hand until the dried sheep droppings glowed, and we absorbed the heat. Men, women, and children would crowd into the tent, all wrapped in their thick *chubas*, sheepskin robes with the fleece inside. I wished for a similar garment. It was -30°F inside a tent at night and we had to keep our tractor's engine idling continuously to prevent its freezing. More livestock would starve, the nomads told us, and this would cause hardship in the coming years. They depended on sheep for meat as well as for wool, which they sold for cash or bartered for tea, *tsamba*—the roasted, ground barley that is a Tibetan staple—and other necessities.

When Russian Colonel Nikolai Przewalski traveled through this area in the 1870s the whole region was uninhabited, no doubt because the land is so unforgiving to those who are unprepared for its vehemence.

He related that "in February 1870 a caravan which left Lhassa [*sic*] 300 strong, with 1,000 beasts of burden, in a violent snow-storm followed by severe cold, lost all the animals and fifty men besides." Its remote location kept the region empty, and its perils kept it beautiful. But a road between Golmud and Lhasa was built during the 1950s, and it brought in pastoralists and other settlers.

These days taught me how precarious, how tenuously balanced on the edge, life is in the Chang Tang. One heavy snowstorm can bring poverty to a nomad family, and wildlife populations can be reduced to such a low level that they may take years to recover. There was hunting for subsistence and profit; the wild yak was already gone from this area. Nomads were now penetrating ever more deeply into steppes that even three decades ago were solely the domain of the wild animals. Any project in the area would have to consider the nomads; only their cooperation and participation could ensure protection of the wildlife.

I was permitted to skirt the edges of the Chang Tang for several years with wildlife surveys in Qinghai and southern Xinjiang, but the heart, the essence, of the Chang Tang in Tibet still eluded me, sealed to foreigners. Chinese scientific expeditions had penetrated, but no Westerner had trod there since 1908, except in 1950 when Fulbright scholar Frank Bessac, Douglas Mackiernan—the American consul in Xinjiang's capital, Urumqi—and

LEFT: After the heaviest snowfall in thirty years covered the eastern Chang Tang on October 17, 1985, my coworkers and I joined a team of Tibetans and Chinese soldiers of the People's Liberation Army to check on the well-being of the nomadic pastoralists who occupy the steppe. In a truck and a tractor-pulled wagon we traveled several hundred miles cross-country. We sometimes broke through the ice of shallow lakes and bogged down in mud hidden below the snow. Within days after the storm, thousands of sheep and goats were starving and had to be slaughtered. Nomads cannot store enough fodder for such crises.

BELOW: Even the inside of a nomad's tent is intensely cold in winter, except around the fire during the day. Family members wear their thick sheepskin *chubas* inside. The long sleeves of a *chuba* cover the hands and keep them warm.

three White Russians fled civil war in Xinjiang by crossing the Chang Tang toward Lhasa. Tibetan border guards killed Mackiernan and two of the Russians but the others reached safety. Memories of the Chang Tang had vanished from the Western world, except for those recorded in the books of long-dead explorers and the mind of Frank Bessac, who was still alive.

I wanted to form a bridge of memory between past and present while the wildlife persisted on this boundless steppe, much of which had never been touched by the hooves or mouths of livestock. No one now alive has seen the American West with its vast bison herds and its prairies unfenced, unplowed, undamaged by sheep and cattle. The Chang Tang must be spared a similar fate. From

hilltops I had gazed far into the Chang Tang, a toneless, gray expanse, a hard land devoid of illusions, austere yet tranquil, seemingly empty but not lonely. I could only agree with Sven Hedin when he wrote, "What a wonderful—what an utterly God-forsaken region this was!" More than ever I wanted to find its heart.

I returned to the Chang Tang's fringes in 1986 and in 1987. After that third trip, I gave a memorandum to the Ministry of Forestry, the Chinese sponsor of my surveys. In it I stated that "plains animals are easily decimated or exterminated. This has been well illustrated by the slaughter of wildlife on the American plains during the second half of the past century. . . . There is a need to protect the area now—before the pressures of development affect it adversely." I suggested that about 150,000 square miles of the Chang Tang be designated as a conservation area in which wildlife is carefully managed and development controlled. Such protection would "emphasize China's commitment to the rational use of its resources, and it will affirm the old local cultural traditions of protecting all life." The officials at the Ministry of Forestry listened politely to my suggestions and read my reports and kept their own counsel about what action, if any, they might take concerning the area and my desire to study wildlife there. But in 1988, using a circuitous bureaucratic route, I finally was permitted to begin work in Tibet's Chang Tang.

My wife, Kay, and I, and our colleagues, approached Tibet from the Xinjiang Autonomous Region in China's far west, up a valley lunar in its desolation between the Kunlun and Karakoram mountains until suddenly, on cresting a ridge, the uplands spread before us, a corrugated landscape of hills and flats. We drove to Rutog, an oasis of barley fields near Panggong Lake, which has islands upon which colonies of brown-headed gulls nest. Heading northeast into the Chang Tang, we passed an arm of Lumajangdong Co (*co, coring,* and *caka* all mean "lake" in Tibetan), crossed the rugged Aru Range, and descended a boulder-strewn glacial stream into a basin. Ahead were the turquoise waters of Aru Co, tranquil beneath pillows of cloud. Wild yaks grazed on a nearby hillside and kiang galloped away at our approach. The grass was green and speckled with flowers: white edelweiss, purple-blossomed legumes, and tiny yellow cinquefoil. I breathed deeply. Here was a place that spoke to the soul, a hidden sanctuary in the depth of the Chang Tang. With imperial restlessness, British travelers had passed through the basin on three occasions—in 1891, 1897, and 1903—but since then no Westerner had beheld it. Our schedule permitted only three days, but Kay and I were determined to return.

From western Tibet we headed to Lhasa, a week's drive, where I made contact with the Tibet Forest Bureau. The help and participation of the bureau's staff made much of my

subsequent work in Tibet possible. When I returned to Lhasa in November the following year, the town was under martial law, the result of clashes between Tibetans and Chinese that spring, and I was not permitted into the field. However, I made a three-year agreement with the Tibet Plateau Institute of Biology for cooperative work with its scientists—the research to focus on the Chang Tang and to begin in 1990 with a return to the Aru Basin. Between 1990 and 1994 I collaborated with the Institute and the Tibet Forest Bureau on six trips to the Chang Tang, each lasting one to three months, for a total of about twelve months. I would have preferred a more intensive long-term field effort, but it was not up to me to determine our schedule. Still, in our journeys we surveyed the wildlife in a large portion of the Chang Tang, obtaining a baseline of information that, I hoped, would help the conservation effort.

As in most field projects, the work went through several stages. At first I explored, collected facts, and sorted impressions, and these then formed the basis for certain specific goals. Wildlife for its own sake remained my passion, but any project must also be concerned with what it leaves behind, how it will benefit the animals. It was my dream that the northern Chang Tang would become a sanctuary where wildlife, livestock, and people lived in harmony. But such a conservation initiative demanded knowledge of the interactions between livestock and wildlife,

Brown-headed gulls nest on islands in some Chang Tang lakes, their eggs and chicks safe from sand foxes and other such mammalian predators. High-altitude birds in summer, they migrate south to spend the winter in estuaries along the coasts of India, Indochina, and southwest China.

Asters, yellow-flowered cinquefoil, and the white blossoms of the cushion plant *Androsace* add a pointillistic touch of color to the terrain.

particularly regarding competition over grazing. Human issues became an integral part of my program, as always, offering both hope and frustration.

I have made a dozen journeys to the Chang Tang—in Qinghai, Xinjiang, and Tibet—each with a distinct purpose, and I have debated how best to present them in this book. One approach would be descriptive, a guidebook with chapters on geography and topography, on wild yaks and other species, on nomads and conservation issues, a tidy and logical presentation. But such an approach would not convey the unpredictable way the work was actually done; it would also leave out what I saw and felt during this intensely personal project. A number of Tibetans and Chinese traveled with me, certain ones as valuable participants and others not, and at least some deserve mention. So I decided on a book of incidents, facts, and feelings, of anecdotes and memories all tied to specific journeys that had only one ultimate goal: to preserve the Chang Tang as part of Tibet's natural and cultural heritage.

The Chang Tang project was conducted under the auspices of the Wildlife Conservation Society in New York, and I thank William Conway and John Robinson for their encouragement. Several donors, especially the Liz Claiborne–Art Ortenberg Foundation, the Robert and Helen Kleberg Foundation, and the Sacharuna Foundation, provided generous support. Without the cooperation of the Tibet Plateau Institute of Biology and the Tibet Forest Bureau, the project would not have been possible. Beijing's Ministry of Forestry and Tibet's Bureau of Science and Technology approved our proposals. The forest bureaus of Qinghai and Xinjiang and the Northwest Institute of Endangered Animals in Xian also participated in the project outside of Tibet. Some of my coworkers are mentioned in the text, but I would like to thank especially Li Hong, Talipu, Ren Junrang, Guo Gieting, Wang Haibin, Qiu Mingjiang, Gu Binyuan, Chi Doa, Ni Zhicheng, Cang Jue Zuoma, Liu Wulin, Daniel Miller, and Ding Li. Whenever one works in an alien place, one needs human intimacy, someone dependable to help, share feelings, relieve strangeness. Kay held such security for me on the many Tibetan trips we shared, just as over the decades we roamed other parts of the world. Whether she is beside me in a tent, deep in her sleeping bag with only her blond hair visible, or awaiting my return in the United States, she is my emotional center. For her devotion, assistance, and companionship, I express my appreciation and love.

June 1987

The kneeling Bactrian camels groaned and squeaked as Abdullah and Kurban lashed tents, bedrolls, boxes, buckets, a dead sheep, sacks of maize, and other items onto their backs. I climbed up on a camel and settled on a folded blanket between his humps. A violent lurch threw me forward as he rose on his hindlegs, and just as abruptly was I propelled backward, barely keeping my seat, as he heaved up on his forelegs. Our camels set off into the morning frost, up the Kökungü Valley in Xinjiang, looking like an ancient trading caravan. Each camel had a stick through its nasal septum like a miniature harpoon, and it was tied to the pack saddle of the animal in front. If a camel failed to keep pace, its nose received a painful tug. Traveling in two sections, one with six camels and the other with ten, we had started at the village of Tula, where the Kunlun Shan (*shan* means "mountain" in Chinese) forks, the Arjin Shan following the plateau's rim and the Kunlun Shan continuing to the southeast. There were eleven of us—four members of the Uygur minority people from Tula and one from the Xinjiang Forest Bureau, four Chinese, my son Mark, and myself.

ABOVE AND OVERLEAF: Our caravan of Bactrian camels moves south across the desolate Kunlun Shan toward the fringe of the Chang Tang. Wild camels, the progenitors of our domestic animals, roamed these hills a century ago, but now fewer than a thousand survive only in a few remote tracts of the Taklimakan and Gobi deserts in China and Mongolia. My son Mark rides the second camel above.

ABOVE: After we crossed the Kunlun Shan, the Tibetan Plateau stretched before us, sparsely covered with a coarse sedge. There is not even a touch of green in early June.

OPPOSITE: We usually camped by midafternoon to rest the camels, which were still lean from winter, and to give me time to explore.

I had asked Tochti, our caravan leader, a dour, chunky Uygur with a limp, why we needed sixteen camels for a three-week trip, and he answered that there was little to eat for the animals on the plateau and that we needed extra ones to carry maize for them. I saw what he meant as we crossed the Kunlun Shan into uninhabited terrain. It was an utterly tired and tan wasteland, so desolate that even birds avoided it. We rode in silence. There was only the wind, the soft scuffle of camel footpads on sand, and the tinkle of a bell. The last camel wears a bell, its ring signaling to the person on the lead camel that all is well, that no animals have detached themselves. The rocking glide of a camel's gait is gentle and the animal needs no guidance. On my high perch I was free to look around, almost free of the earth, seeing the landscape as might a low-flying bird. A raven

passed overhead, the first bird I had seen all day, an incident worth noting in my journal. The terrain ahead leveled and we broke out of the mountains and onto the plateau. Ahead were low hills and alkali flats rolling south into the depths of the Chang Tang. Six chiru fled, pale ephemeral creatures afloat in heat waves.

This is the way to travel, not encased in a vehicle, but exposed to the elements, living the landscape slowly. A biologist's curiosity had prompted this journey, but it also re-created a world when explorers headed into the unknown beyond the security of their culture, solely responsible for their own lives, and I found atavistic pleasure in this personal engagement with the past. Nikolai Przewalski and Pyotr Kozlov with their band of armed cossacks had crisscrossed this region just over a hundred years before. Prince Henry of Orleans and Gabriel Bonvalot had headed south from here in 1889, the first Westerners to cross the Chang Tang in that direction. Sven Hedin came this way in 1891, Jules Dutreuil de Rhins and Fernand Grenard in 1893 (de Rhins was killed by Tibetans on that trip), and the Englishman St. George Littledale with a caravan that included his wife and terrier in 1895. All entered through Tibet's back door, from Xinjiang, starting as we did at the edge of the fierce desert called Taklimakan, a Turkic word meaning "enter and you will not come out." Like us they crossed the Arjin Shan and Kunlun Shan and used Muztag, a 22,875-foot ice mountain on

the Tibet border, as their beacon. They crossed the Chang Tang, but the Tibetan army near Siling Co denied them their goal, forbidden Lhasa. Western presence has been brief and transient here, a mere crumb of history, its memory lingering in old books and topographical tributes to obscure persons on forgotten maps. And then as now the land was unpeopled, without roads, houses, even nomads.

The only vegetation here at fifteen thousand feet was a few *Ceratoides* shrubs, browsed down to ground level, and patches of a coarse sedge. Yet the region had wildlife. We had seen several chiru, and now off to one side were the massive, curled horns and a few bones of a Tibetan argali sheep. Perhaps a wolf dropping too, I thought, but I was too far away to be certain. I was "riding a horse to look at flowers," to use a Chinese expression indicating a fleeting glimpse. I needed to get off the camel and walk to bring me closer to the earth, to enable me to examine, measure, evaluate. An awkward leap, a jarring landing, and I was free of my four-legged impediment. Mark joined me, and we hiked near the caravan, our speed similar to the camels'.

In midafternoon we came to a mud-brown glacial stream and decided to camp. When the camels disdained the local sedges, still dry and yellow this early in June, the herders placed maize on two tarps. Crowding around as if on a picnic, the camels crunched kernels, snorting and spraying mucus from their floppy lips. Yang Mingzhong, our cook,

gathered yak chips and bits of root and brewed tea, a cutbank protecting the fire from wind. Li Hong, our leader, a tall, lean, and enthusiastic man, started a card game, which several of the team joined. Racheman strummed his mandolin-like *reawap*. I climbed a nearby hill. To the south, beyond the plains, the double peak of Muztag, a shimmer of white suspended in the sky; below, our tents and camels lost in the immensity of the land. I have a covenant with such scenes. Dinner was noodles and mutton, the remains of a Tula sheep. When the sun dipped behind the hills and the shadows seeped up the slopes like a tide, summer abruptly became winter, and we withdrew into our sleeping bags. The camels kneeled in a row, tied together. The squealing

Himalayan marmots favor alpine meadows with lush vegetation near their burrows, a scarce habitat in this part of the Tibetan Plateau. Since marmots hibernate for six months or more, they need to build up large fat reserves during the four-month growing season. Adult marmots weigh ten to fifteen pounds, a substantial meal for a bear, lynx, wolf, or snow leopard. Litters usually contain four to six young, two of which are shown here at their burrow entrance.

roars of a spat. *"Chuka, chuka,"* Lie down, called an Uygur to the camels into the dusk.

We soon developed a rhythm of travel and camping. But the weather did not settle into a pattern. Serene sun gave way to sudden violent storms, the wind abrading our skin with snow and sand whipping horizontally like shrapnel. The camels plodded on. We sat with shoulders hunched, legs frozen in place, minds drawn inward. Mark said he planned meals and experiments in social psychology, which is his profession. The camels were molting and the wind tore away strips of wool, slowly unraveling the animals and leaving their gray skin naked. The head of my camel, with his woolly cap of hair supported by his nude neck, bobbed before me like that of a grotesque bird. After staring at that movement for hours, my mind emptied. The camels shivered at times from cold; we were not kind to bring them here at this season.

My field notes were as spartan as the environment. A pair of ruddy shelduck in an alkaline pool; a brown bear track; several chiru females, their abdomens bulging, the time of birth near. Old kiang and wild yak droppings showed that the animals had been here earlier. Perhaps they had moved east to lower elevations and nutritious green grass in the spring. Wolves canvased these uplands for prey, leaving their droppings as prominent calling cards at mountain passes and the base of cliffs. I hoped for a glimpse of these predators but they, too, were elsewhere.

I collected a sample of wolf droppings in a plastic bag, and later, after we established camp, I checked their contents. There was the soft fleece of chiru and sometimes a hoof, the stiff blue-gray hairs of blue sheep, and most commonly the coarse hair and fragile bones of marmots. I was pleased to be in wolf country; there are so few places in China where the predators have a chance to survive. Pastoralists detest them, anyone with a gun shoots them on sight, and reserves offer no protection because even there wolves are considered outlaws. With everyone against them in this part of the world, only biologists like myself seem to appreciate their role in nature, admire their beauty, speak kindly of them; we have become their spirit owners.

We traveled on for hours and days, swinging east, yet seemingly staying in place except that the snows of Muztag were no longer ahead but to our right. Once, as I roamed on foot, the caravan stopped and Li Hong waved to me. A dead marmot was by its hole, bloody and belly-up. Someone said *sheli*, lynx, and at that moment a tawny cat trotted up a nearby slope, its pale coat blending into the background except for the bobbing stump of its black tail. Then a second lynx fled. I did not handle the marmot: plague, the bacterial infection transmitted by fleas from rodents, is endemic to Xinjiang. I hoped the cats would soon return to their meal.

An apron of grass spread along the base of a low hill range where we found a spring,

OVERLEAF: Wild yaks are supremely well adapted to the Chang Tang. A dense layer of wool beneath the long guard hairs keeps them so warm that even on brisk days they may stand in ice-cold streams to cool off. Their blood cells are about half the size of those in cattle, and there are at least three times more of them per unit volume, increasing the blood's capacity to carry oxygen at high altitudes. A male such as this may weigh 1200–1800 pounds, averaging a third more than a female.

It was a delicious feeling, to know that we were the first human beings to tread these mountains, where there existed no path, where there never had been a path, and where there was not a footprint visible, except those made by the hoof of yak, antelope, or kulan [kiang]. It was a no man's land; rivers, lakes, and mountains were all nameless; their shores, banks, and snow fields had never been seen by any traveller's eyes but mine; they were mine own kingdom of a day. It was delightful—it was a great thing to cruise, like a vessel that leaves no track behind her, amongst those upwellings of the world's "high sea," to make our way over those gigantic mountain waves. Only the waves which roll across the Tibetan highlands are petrified; and all distances and dimensions are cast on such a gigantic scale, that you may march for weeks at a time and still find the situation unchanged—still find yourself the centre of a universe of mountains. I felt like an atom of dust in the midst of the illimitable wastes, and fancied I could hear the swish of the planet as it rolled without rest, without cessation, along its everlasting orbit.

—Sven Hedin
Through Asia, 1903

and we set up camp so that the camels could eat. Still in poor condition after a long winter, the camels needed rest and food, and the Uygurs wanted to take them back to Tula. We had a late lunch of tea and *nan*, a bagel-like bread. The *nan* was rock-hard, and we could eat it only by smashing it with stones and soaking the pieces in our tea. As usual, the wind was raw and relentless, the terrain offering no place to hide. A few days before, gusts had tumbled Mark's tent with him in it, shredded the fly on mine, and threatened to carry the tent away until Yang Mingzhong dumped a sack of maize in with me to provide extra weight. At least the snow squalls were now temporarily over. The plains were hazy with dust from the Taklimakan Desert.

Our camp was just west of the Qiemo River. Beyond the river is the Arjin Shan Nature Reserve, 17,325 square miles in size, established as a national reserve in 1985, and managed by the National Environmental Protection Agency. But because we were here on behalf of the Forest Bureau, we were prohibited from entering the reserve. Competition between the two departments was as relentless as its reasons were obscure. In a gesture of acute paranoia the agency had even sent a vehicle from Urumqi to Tula, over 650 miles, to check on us.

There was grass near our camp and it had attracted wildlife. I meandered over the landscape to collect kiang, chiru, and other droppings. Using a technique that not only identifies in the droppings what kind of plants an animal has eaten but also approximately how much of each (plant species have characteristic cell structures and these can be observed under the microscope), I could obtain valuable information on food habits without in any way affecting the animals. Leisurely tasks, such as collecting an animal's artifacts, give the most pleasure afield because the mind is more receptive to small and insignificant encounters. I found an old yak skull, a bull with frayed horns, sand drifted up to its orbits. As Loren Eiseley has noted, "Every bone that one holds in one's hands is a fallen kingdom . . . a unique object that will never return through time." A sand fox had placed a dropping tidily on the skull's forehead; in this way the yak had achieved reincarnation in the fox's world. To the fox the skull had important dimensions as a landmark and signpost, a place of identity in this immense space. The fox had given me a lesson in geography: its universe and mine were different.

I was disappointed that we had seen only thirteen wild yaks so far on this trip, most of them solitary bulls and all of them shy. Climbing over a rise, I came upon a black boulder, a yak bull in repose. I was alone, and he was not afraid, no more than he would be of a lone wolf. When I strolled to within about a hundred feet of him, he rose to his feet with his armored head facing me. His long mantle of hair almost reached the ground, obscuring his feet. He had the aura of a Stonehenge dolmen in a land of power and magic.

Leaving the bull in peace, I walked toward the river flats where I had seen several chiru. From the lee of a hillock I observed five males below me. They were in their drab summer coat, buff-colored with gray on the muzzle. Their ringed and lyrate horns, rising almost two feet, gave them their unique and elegant appearance. They grazed and intermittently asserted rank. One would arch his neck so far down that his muzzle almost touched the ground. With stiletto-tipped horns pointing forward, he would then walk stiffly past another male, intimidating him until he turned aside.

A journey such as this seemed to yield relatively little information. At the end, after nearly three weeks, my notebook showed a tally of 438 chiru, 108 kiang, 24 argali sheep, 14 yaks, and 4 Tibetan gazelles as well as a few blue sheep, sand foxes, marmots, and various birds. I had collected plants and droppings and analyzed the diet of wolves. In this day of sophisticated research, I remained a nineteenth-century wanderer with a naturalist's bent, little different from Nikolai Przewalski, who made the wild Bactrian camel, white-lipped deer, and black-necked crane, among other species on the Tibetan Plateau, known to science. Yet ideas, concepts, and plans are built upon basic knowledge and even such a brief survey trip provided useful insights. Wildlife was scarce, at least at this season, but it had become clear to me that animals moved in and out of the Arjin Shan Reserve; the reserve needed to be expanded westward. Did wildlife move north into this region from the Tibetan Chang Tang?

We turned back toward Tula by a route different from the one that had brought us. I felt a sense of loss at leaving; I wanted to head south past Muztag deeper into the Chang Tang. But there is a circle to life, of sun and seasons, of Himalayan griffon vultures spiraling in updrafts, of wolves eating marmots, of returning to Tula. And I would come back to the Chang Tang.

July and August 1990

We had only the Aru Range left to cross before reaching the Aru Basin. Having reached the small Yarlung Basin, we were trying to find our 1988 route, but snow clouds were low on the peaks, obscuring the pass, and our truck, laden with gasoline barrels and food for a month, often bogged down in this trackless terrain. None of the ten Tibetans and Chinese from the Tibet Plateau Institute of Biology had been here before. We set up camp at 16,900 feet beside a rivulet. Seventy-six wild yaks left a grass swale above

ABOVE: Gu Binyuan (left) and Chi Doa (right), our trip leaders, ask directions at a nomad camp.

PRECEDING PAGES: Summer in the Chang Tang.

us and moved into cloud. That night the wind raged and snow pelted the tent; tucked deep into our sleeping bags, Kay and I worried that our anemic truck might not be able to cross the range, a barrier our two Land Cruisers could easily surmount.

Snow and cloud still whipped along the ground at dawn. Two of our team had headaches and felt nauseous from the altitude. We had breakfast at noon, a rice soup made in a pressure cooker heated with a gasoline-fueled blowtorch, our usual stove. When the clouds briefly lifted, I went on foot toward an adjoining valley to look for the route to the pass. Less than a mile from camp, I saw two inert humps in swirling cloud. Moving closer, I distinguished two *drokba*, as the nomadic herders call themselves, wrapped in their sheepskin robes and wearing traditional high cloth boots. They hunched over a smoldering yak-dung fire making tea. A muzzle loader lay on the ground between them. "*Tashiy delay*," Hello, I greeted them and squatted by the fire. They nodded casually in return as if they often met foreigners here. One of the men spoke a little Chinese, and from him I learned that heavy rains the previous year had made the route to the pass impassable but that there was another way about forty kilometers to the northwest. It was a strange interlude by that fire, three men of today's world, yet all of us still antique people; they leading in part the traditional nomad's life of ages past and I a seeker from

the West penetrating the unknown in the steps of Sven Hedin.

The following day we found a vague track, but it ceased at a tent where a truck was picking up sheared wool. Until recently a nomad had to travel for weeks by yak caravan to trade his wool in town for barley and other necessities. Now motorized traders reach the most distant families. Yes, we were told, the route from here to the Aru Basin is easy, just up that valley beyond. The ascent to the pass was gradual, and on top were the heads of two wild yaks encased in shriveled skin, the discarded trophies of a meat hunter. And soon Aru Co was before us again.

We established camp by a clear stream, a rarity here where silt-laden meltwater from the glaciers usually makes water turbid. A large cook tent was our communal room, and most of our Tibetan coworkers also slept in it. Several other smaller tents provided the rest of us with nighttime retreats, the three vehicles pulled close as defense against the elements.

The last day of July. Dawn was at 8 AM—Tibet retained Beijing time in spite of being several time zones away—and the temperature was 23°F. I was eager for fieldwork, to census wildlife, study vegetation, satisfy a passion to understand. I rose with the sun and climbed a slope that offered a wide view. The Aru Basin is constructed on a grand scale, about fifty miles long and up to fifteen miles wide, bordered on the west by the Aru Range, several of its peaks over twenty thousand feet high. From the crest of the range the terrain plunges to an alluvial plain which descends gradually to the margins of two lakes, Aru Co and Memar Co. Rounded hills, usually no higher than seventeen thousand feet, embrace the basin on its other sides. Such description cannot convey the enchantment of the place. Hidden here in the Chang Tang is a haven where human intrusion has been brief, where wolf families can raise their cubs, and yak herds spread over golden pastures. Here lakes absorb color from the deep-blue sky and glaciers shine among surging peaks, filling the basin with waves of light. Mountains often exalt, but here they lift your spirit and keep it afloat.

Camp remained silent that morning. I was not allowed to take a car out alone and had to wait, but at least I could freely wander. Black-lipped pikas, those tailless rat-sized relatives of rabbits, scurried about in the morning sun, and Brandt's mountain finches sought seeds among the tussocks. Still camp slept on, except for Kay, who strolled nearby in search of alpine flowers. Finally a faint stir at 10 AM. An hour later the Tibetans had their buttered tea and *tsamba* while the Chinese drifted around camp. Breakfast for the Chinese, Kay, and me: a dish of stir-fried luncheon meat, peas, and chili peppers, which congealed as the rice cooked. It was nearly 2 PM before camp was ready to begin the day's work. When I indicated my frustration at such a schedule, I was told: "We talk at night and eat and sleep during the day." And, based on our trip so far, he might have added, often drink virulent *bai jiu*, a raw liquor, to excess. However, on all trips I had to remind myself that Kay and I sought out these wild and lonesome uplands, whereas they, Chinese and Tibetans alike, preferred urban comforts. To them camping was not pleasure but unnecessary hardship in a dangerous place which they had been ordered to endure.

Our leader was Gu Binyuan, an intense chain-smoker, who was often in a "reflective

Kiang stallions are often alone or in small bachelor herds. They do not form a permanent family bond with mares.

mood," as a team member jokingly called his disengagement. He successfully resisted scientific involvement, but he was always determined to achieve our goals, and for that I liked his participation on this and subsequent journeys. An unsuitable person may affect the tone of an entire team, and unfortunately we were accompanied by an obsessively loud photographer for China Central Television. I found him particularly irritating, in part because he had purchased snow leopard skins in Rutog and also avidly collected chiru horns which, I was told, he planned to sell later in Lhasa. These illegal activities reflected badly on us all. We disliked each other without displaying it. Most team members devoted themselves to killing time, to sharing each other's boredom. Zhang Yaozung, a young assistant at the institute, was keen to assist Kay and me until his initiative was criticized by his coworkers. In spite of this we maintained a compulsive harmony. In the evenings Kay and I particularly enjoyed the spontaneity of Dashi—a vigorous driver who considered obstructions to be relative abstractions —Chi Doa, and Cang Jue Zuoma, all Tibetans who sang and laughed and included us in their banter.

That first afternoon, Xiong Jigui, a patient and careful driver, Zhang Yaozung, and I drove south in the Aru Basin along the base of the hills, around and through gullies, across gravel outwashes and occasionally across smooth flats covered with *Stipa*, or

feather grass, the dominant species here on the steppe. Scattered along our route were kiang, often solitary stallions, standing erect as if posted on guard duty. Small herds of two or three mares wandered through the area. The stallions seemed to be on territories in which other males were unwelcome but mares desired. Sometimes, fleeing from our car, one stallion entered another's area and was promptly pursued by the resident, the latter's head held high with ears laid back. But if mares came, he pranced around them, trying to induce them to stay. I made a mental note to observe their behavior more closely. Besides, I enjoyed watching them, handsome in their chestnut coats and gleaming white undersides. They were often curious, more so than other species. Sometimes a lone kiang or even a herd raced alongside our car, one mile, three miles, as if keeping an eye on us, or just

ABOVE: Two kiang mares, possibly a mother with her grown daughter, are shedding their woolly winter coats in July. Kiang mate in summer and give birth a year later. Consequently a mare will have a foal at most once every two years.

RIGHT: A kiang herd races our vehicle at 30 mph. The kiang is the only one of the wild ungulate species in the Chang Tang Reserve that may be locally increasing. I would estimate that around twenty-five thousand kiang exist in the reserve.

from an untamed compulsion to race. Whatever the reason, to observe these sleek animals
galloping across the steppe, their tasseled
tails streaming in the wind, is to behold one
of the primal visions of the Chang Tang.

We rounded a spur, the Aru Basin retreated, and we had a view of the slopes sweeping
up past the limit of vegetation to the everlasting snows. Black dots speckled an upper
slope. Wild yaks. Excitedly I attached my
spotting scope to the tripod and began to
count: a hundred animals, including five
calves, most at rest in ponderous ease. Nearby
were twenty-three more yaks with four calves
crossing a snow field at about eighteen thousand feet. These and several more brought
the total to 152. I remembered that Captain
M. Wellby, a British officer and the first
Westerner to cross the Chang Tang west to
east in 1896, once came upon a hill on which
"we could see hundreds upon hundreds of
yak grazing; there was, I believe, more yak
visible than hill." The slope before me
seemed frozen in time. There were three
golden yaks in the herd, including a black
cow with a golden calf and a golden cow with
a black calf, the contrast between mother and
offspring startling. This golden color was
rare, the recessive gene or genes appearing in
only 1 to 2 percent of the animals.

During the following days we censused
yaks in the whole basin, counting a total of
681. There were lone bulls, bachelor herds,
and mixed herds of cows with youngsters and

ABOVE: Wild yaks file up a slope, one golden
animal strikingly conspicuous among them.
Many domestic yaks have patches of white or
other color patterns, but the wild golden yaks
of the Aru region are unique.

OPPOSITE: A herd of wild yaks—mostly
cows, subadults, and a few calves—idles
on a slope of the Aru Range. Most adult
bulls remain solitary or in small bachelor
herds for much of the year.

usually two to three huge bulls with horns sweeping out, forward, then up and in for three feet. The yaks were not innocent of vehicles, having learned that death may follow their appearance. Some fled when our car was still a mile away, the animals bunching into a dense mass as if herded by wolves. They lumbered upslope toward the snows where the herd unraveled until it became a strand of black beads draped across the mountain.

The Aru Basin was like a miniature Serengeti, the national park in Tanzania where Kay and I had studied lions for several years. The yaks were the equivalent of buffalo, the kiang of zebra, the chiru of the migratory wildebeest, and the Tibetan gazelles of Thomson's gazelles. Above all, in both places

there were always animals in view, always something that touched mind and heart. For several hours each day, Xiong Jigui drove Kay and me and anyone else who wanted to come to different parts of the basin where we counted herds and classified animals by age and sex. Among the easiest to tally were the sprightly gazelles. They were alone or in small herds, seldom more than a dozen, and since only the males have horns it was easy to distinguish the sexes. Gazelles have a large, heart-shaped rump patch whose white hairs fan out conspicuously when the animal is excited, a heliograph that flashes its code across the steppe.

At times I abandoned the car, took my scope, and wandered to a distant hillock. There I settled myself just below the crest, below where grass met sky, so that I blended in, and I counted animals at leisure. A favorite place was near the southern end of Memar Co. From where I sat old beach lines were clearly visible showing that lake levels in the past few thousand years had been at least 130 feet higher. Only one large lake extended the whole length of the basin at that time. The lakes and peaks in this peaceful basin seemed eternal, but the beach lines told of a turbulent past. At the height of the last ice age, about eighteen thousand years ago, glaciers from the Aru Range flowed far into the basin. As, in recent millennia, the summers became warmer and winters colder, reducing snowfall, glaciers melted and water levels rose.

Except during the January–February rut, adult male Tibetan gazelles tend to remain separate from the females. The smallest of the six wild ungulate species in the Chang Tang Reserve, gazelles weigh only thirty to thirty-five pounds.

Male chiru live segregated from the females for much of the year. When the females migrate to the calving grounds, the males loiter in various parts of the reserve, concentrating in some places such as the Aru Basin. A male weighs about eighty-five to ninety pounds, as compared to the fifty-five-pound female.

The basin must have been an inhospitable place. But the climate then became drier and lakes shrank as their waters evaporated under the intense solar radiation, opening up new habitat for yaks and chiru. I was a witness to the last of the Pleistocene.

On an alkali flat near the lake stood many male chiru in a compact herd. Viscous heat waves engulfed their bodies but their massed horns reached clear sky. The animals looked like one great spiny creature submerged just below the surface of the sea. I could not count them but estimated about a hundred. Why did they stand there as if they worshiped light? I had noticed that the basin held almost exclusively males. Where were the females?

I have spoken little of chiru so far, yet they intrigued me more than any other creature in the Chang Tang. As a boy I had seen photographs of dead chiru in the books of explorers who shot them for food. "I have fired as many as one to two hundred shots at them in the course of a day," wrote Nikolai Przewalski, a testament either to his marksmanship or appetite. Visions of chiru had floated in my mind for years. They look as if they have somehow strayed from the African plains—their lanky legs seem designed for striding toward the horizon, and their large, bright eyes are ideal for sweeping the steppe for danger.

Hundreds of males idled away the summer in the Aru Basin. I wondered why they assembled on barren flats, or at times on sheets of overflow ice in streambeds. I remembered seeing caribou in Alaska gathered in such a way, hiding in a crowd from mosquitoes, warble flies, and other noxious insects. The Chang Tang lacks mosquitoes but there are warble flies, which look like squat bees. The fly lays eggs on an animal's legs, and, after hatching, the larvae cut into and migrate below the skin to the lower back. There each makes a breathing hole in the skin and lives until the following spring when it escapes through that hole and soon pupates on the ground. That at least is the cycle in caribou and it probably is in chiru too. I examined several dead chiru; their backs were riddled with holes, and a few larvae were still in residence—dark, cor-

45

rugated grubs three-quarters of an inch long. Occasionally a warble fly landed on my head and burrowed into my hair, but I did not permit it to continue its life cycle.

Sometimes when I crossed an expanse of steppe, empty and without shadows, a chiru popped from the earth as if from a subterranean abode. The animals pawed hollows about three feet in diameter and up to a foot deep, private scattered retreats in which they crouched. Past explorers assumed that chiru hide from wind and predators, and the hollows could indeed serve that function, but I ultimately concluded that chiru conceal themselves from cruising warble flies.

In months of roaming the plateau, I had never seen the Tibetan brown bear, which, based on skull measurements and distinctive coat color, is a separate subspecies. I had examined the bears' droppings, with their two-inch bore, and noted that they contained mainly grass, roots, and pikas; and I had seen where an animal had dug into rocky soil in pursuit of marmots. Such melancholy leavings of a rare creature. Nomads regard bears with dread because they are dangerous, prey on livestock, and are considered manifestations of evil spirits; bear gallbladders are also prized in traditional medicines. For all these reasons the bears are targets for anyone with a gun. What a terrible fate it must be for a bear to be the last in a region searching for a mate and finding none, not a track, not a scent. I had often focused my scope on a distant bear

only to discover yet another rock. Better stop thinking bear and speaking bear, I told myself, and perhaps one will appear.

And within a few days of our arrival in the Aru Basin I saw one at last, a small animal, perhaps three and a half years old. When it heard the car it stood bolt upright, straining its senses, trying to validate its unease. It was strikingly colored, with black legs and ears, a face and body the color of dead grass, and a broad, white collar; its ears had shaggy tassels, giving it a clownish face. The bear bounded toward Aru Co. Driver Xiong was delighted with this meeting because in Chinese one meaning of *xiong* is "bear."

A few days later, as Xiong and Kay drove toward camp, a bear rushed at them from a dip in the plain, her head threateningly low, hair bristling, and with utter fury chased the car, then chased twice more when they paused at a distance. Xiong accelerated faster than usual.

"I have never, ever, seen such an angry animal," Kay told me later. It was a female with two small cubs.

After these encounters I remained alert for bears when I was afoot. Like mountain spirits they followed me on all my solitary wanderings. The risk of a mishap was low, yet there could be no escape from an irascible bear: the highest tree in the Chang Tang, a procumbent *Myricaria* with its main branches underground, is a few inches tall.

Not all my time was devoted to large mammals: Kay and I spent days on our hands

Most lakes in Tibet were formed between the last two ice ages, about thirty thousand years ago. After the last ice age, which reached its peak twelve thousand years ago, lakes evaporated in the dry climate and intense sun, leaving most of those that remained brackish. Old beach lines reveal former lake levels. As shown in this photograph, the level of holy Tangra Yumco, just south of the reserve, was once about 700 feet higher than it is today.

and knees in pursuit of plants, making an inventory, measuring abundance. I had brought a wooden frame with ten pins, like knitting needles, mounted in a line. We stretched a string, marked at two-meter intervals, along a selected site, placed the frame at each indicated spot, and lowered the pins carefully into the vegetation. A hit on a plant was recorded whenever a pin touched a plant. We recorded the species and whether it was alive or dead, grazed or ungrazed. We clipped vegetation from one-square-meter plots and weighed each species, fresh and dried, to determine the amount of food available to herbivores, and we stored samples for later analyses of protein and minerals.

Our work provided us with a useful background about the habitat. The soil was mostly silt and clay, slightly alkaline with a pH of seven to eight. Plant cover was only about 25 percent, mostly grasses and sedges and a few herbs, especially legumes and species growing in dense cushions. Variety was small, often no more than twenty or so species in an area, and biomass was low, our clip plots averaging only about an ounce of dry grass and a fraction of an ounce of herbs each. However, an herbivore there can usually find ample food in terms of quantity—but not necessarily quality, nutritious food high enough in protein, carbohydrates, and minerals to maintain itself and reproduce.

The greatest pleasure for Kay and me came not from collecting such facts but from lingering in this alpine garden. There were blue asters, pink polygonum, white *Ajuga*— plants similar to those growing around our Connecticut home. On rocky hillsides were cushion plants from silver-leafed edelweiss and an *Oxytropis*, whose pods the chiru liked to eat, to a fleshy red *Rhodiola*, a relative of the sedums. Kay, who loves gardening, wondered if they could survive in more temperate climates. A raven croaked. Ravens have a special compact with people, as they do with wolves; these birds consider the activities of both species worth monitoring because they may provide scraps of food at unpredictable intervals. We were happy here, our hearts and surroundings in balance.

One day, I told Gu Binyuan that I would climb into the Aru Range to look for blue sheep. The weather looked good, except for the dark distant curtain of a snow squall. I angled up a slope, soon breathing hard in the thin air, until I reached a crest with a view up a canyon. Settled among boulders, I scanned the terrain. Blue sheep are devoted to the vicinity of cliffs, which offer them escape from wolves. Slate-blue in color, the animals become almost invisible when at rest. I could not spot any but really did not care because it was such a pagan pleasure to

I heat water with fuel tablets to make a cup of cocoa.

RIGHT: Several species of *Saussurea* (top) grow on high rocky ridges, usually above 16,500 feet. Woolly-haired leaves protect them from cold and desiccation in this lofty, dry terrain. Multicolored lichens (center) splotch some rock faces like miniature abstract murals. The red-berried *Ephedra* (bottom) is one of several species of low to procumbent shrubs in the Chang Tang.

Kay clips a vegetation plot to measure plant biomass on the floor of the Aru Basin. The sparse plant cover here consists mostly of sedge, feather grass, and silver-leafed cushions of edelweiss.

be here. A storm was over Aru Co, the lake dark except for a shaft of light through a fissure of cloud. Our tents were far below, mere specks on the earth's crust. I continued up along the ridge toward the edge of the sky, free, free to be a pika or blue sheep or cloud dancer.

Once more I halted, and still the blue sheep remained elusive. But gliding along the opposite slope on an eight-foot wingspan was a lämmergeyer, or bearded vulture. It banked and came past, the air whispering in its pinions, a red eye focused on me, evaluating, then sailed on, its movements pure visual music. This is where my spirit belongs, I thought, suspended between earth and sky. In his poem "Vulture," Robinson Jeffers wrote:

> To be eaten by that beak and become
> a part of him, to share those wings
> and those eyes—
> What a sublime end of one's body, what an
> enskyment; what a life after death.

A gust of wind and a lash of hail. I hurried down, but, a quarter hour later, by the time I reached the canyon floor the storm had passed and now roiled among the peaks. A blue sheep skull, that of a male, was among the river rocks, his smooth horns curving out back and up; from the number of horn rings I deduced that he was nine years old at death, a respectable age. Perhaps a snow leopard had killed him, or more likely a wolf.

The cold hit hard as soon as the earth turned away from the sun. Crowded into the cook tent we ate hurriedly and then sought the warmth of our sleeping bags. Kay and I read a few minutes by flashlight until our hands got too cold. I looked out of the tent. Formless and black, the Aru Range tilted toward us beneath dark clouds that spoke of snow, and later we heard the flakes rustling on the roof. Even summers in the Chang Tang are perpetual reminders of winter.

The next morning, August 11, was bleak, the steppe hidden in snow, but the sun soon melted it. We had planned to explore the northern rim of the basin. Impatient with the camp's inertia, I left instructions with Kay to pick me up later and left on foot. In the mornings the basin seems gentle in the soft light, its green-gray hues flowing one into another, the roll of the plain almost intimate. Lack of wind suffuses the landscape with a welcome stillness. We had found a wolf den in an old lake terrace only fifteen miles away, and I wanted to examine the site and if possible observe the wolves. There were eight of them, including several lanky red-brown youngsters which now used the den only as a rendezvous. But I lingered near a herd of thirty-two yaks, and the Land Cruiser came before I reached the den.

Near the northern tip of the basin is a plain, a former bed of Memar Co. On it I saw a strange tan, almost pinkish, mass. As my mind groped for a memory, it conjured a mirage of flamingos on a lake in the Chilean

The blue-gray pelage of blue sheep blends so well into the somber hillsides that the animals may be difficult to spot. This resting blue sheep is an adult male, and a female and young are nearby.

Andes. But these were chiru, about two thousand of them, all females and young. The females had vanished from the region, probably to the north, to give birth, and now they were back. Over half of the females had a young at heel.

The trip back to camp was long and rough, but I dwelled on the sight of that chiru herd. Gu Binyuan gave me permission to spend time with them. Taking only Xiong Jigui, Zhang Yaozung, and Kay, I went back two days later. The chiru were scattered over the high rounded hills at about seventeen thousand feet along the northern rim of the basin; they had not moved south through the basin as I had expected. I roamed near them that afternoon, counting, observing, as they foraged on alpine pastures already tinted in autumn yellow. The slant of the sun gave the mountain a gunmetal sheen, a glow as if from an inner light. By the time I returned to our spartan camp—a tent for Kay and me, and the two others slept in the car—clouds had descended. That night and far into the next day it snowed again. At intervals we thumped the sagging tent roof from the inside and listened to the swish of sliding snow. Kay heated each of us a cup of cocoa on fuel tablets brought for just such days. Weather and food seemed to rule our minds and actions in the field. Toward noon the snow stopped, but cloud and land were still merged into one. Chiru tracks etched patterns in the void. The silhouettes of two wolves passed like spirit

dreams, never to be seen again, but later their howls dispelled the astral silence.

We gathered more information that day and the next, and then returned to base, our time over. On August 18 we left the basin, going south and then east. We left with scattered facts, many questions, and a distinct goal. Many chiru females and young were along our route. I wondered why they had bypassed the basin. The chiru were migrating, and I had to trace their routes. How many migratory populations are there in the Chang Tang? It puzzled me that females trekked somewhere to give birth and then immediately returned.

Unhampered migrations by large mammals are vanishing from this earth as humankind fences and plows the land and kills the animals. Saiga antelopes and Mongolian gazelles in Asia, wildebeest and white-eared kob in Africa, caribou in North America—these are some of the great migrations, and all are under threat. The chiru had long ago adapted to this realm, needing a certain space to roam and special places to give birth and spend the winter. My goal now was to make certain that they could retain their pact with solitude.

OPPOSITE AND ABOVE: Chiru females and young skirt the
Aru Basin on their southward migration, traveling together
in herds of hundreds and even a thousand or more.

OVERLEAF: Chiru meander over the plains in search of
forage after an October blizzard. To raise an offspring,
chiru females must overcome nature's obstacles, including
pitiless weather, poor food, long migrations, disease, and
insect harassment. Usually at least half of the young die
within the first few months of life.

Over a pass 17,876 feet, and then down a long
narrow valley which suddenly debouches on Lake
Aru Cho (17,150 feet),—a fine sheet of water running
north and south, salt like nearly all the Tibetan
lakes, and of a deep blue colour. To the south-west
and north-west some fine snowy mountains
rise up into the blue sky, while on the east low
undulating barren-looking hills are seen. In every
direction antelope and yak in incredible numbers
were seen, some grazing, some lying down. No
trees, no signs of man, and this peaceful-looking
lake, never before seen by a European eye,
seemingly given over as a happy grazing ground
to the wild animals. A sportsman's paradise.

—Hamilton Bower
Diary of a Journey Across Tibet, 1894

June and July 1991

After my surveys in 1988 and 1990, I discussed the need for a reserve with the Tibet Forest Bureau, and we also considered potential reserve boundaries and options for managing livestock and wildlife. The creation of a reserve is a complicated political process, needing the cooperation of forestry, agriculture, military, and other departments. However, the government of the Tibet Autonomous Region was then becoming seriously concerned about conservation, and in December 1990 it approved in principle the establishment of a Chang Tang Nature Reserve. It would

encompass about ninety-two thousand square miles, the whole northeastern Chang Tang north of Siling Co. The reserve would be under the jurisdiction of the Tibet Forest Bureau and policed by thirty guards with posts at such communities as Shuanghu and Nyima. My organization, the Wildlife Conservation Society in New York, agreed to provide two patrol vehicles. The commitment by Tibet was impressive, but in my opinion the planned reserve did not extend west far enough to protect the Aru Basin and the important chiru population there. I needed to return to Tibet to lobby for an expansion of the reserve before legal boundaries became established. Also, I wanted to continue the wildlife surveys.

Fieldwork in the Chang Tang was pure pleasure compared to getting there. I could be accused of scientific masochism, enjoying a penance of snow, wind, and high altitude to provide the chiru or other obscure species with a brief biography. But consider the pre-liminaries: after our 1990 trip, the Tibet Plateau Institute of Biology and I agreed to trace the route of migrating chiru in the eastern Chang Tang to the calving grounds. I arrived in Beijing on May 14 to pick up my research permit from the Ministry of Forestry. The institute had not even applied for a permit. Our work needed approval from the Tibet Forest Bureau, the military, and other government departments in Tibet before the ministry could act. The project's

Land Cruiser, which my organization had donated to the institute, was in use elsewhere. I became obstinately patient in pursuit of the permit. Although I received the mushroom treatment—kept in the dark with a lot of manure—I finally received a permit and on June 11, after a wasted month, flew southwest to Chengdu. With luck I might just reach the chiru before their birth peak. But flights from Chengdu to Lhasa were full, bookings as usual in random chaos, and it was not until June 17 that I reached Lhasa.

Three days later we left in a Land Cruiser and truck, seven of us, up out of the lowlands on a paved road to Nagqu, a town at 14,500 feet near the eastern edge of the Chang Tang. It was and still is a major trading center in the region. When Dutreuil de Rhins and Fernand Grenard passed through town in 1894 it consisted of sixty houses and gave an "impression of shabby dreariness." The place was now much larger, as was the impression it made. Loudspeakers brayed, dust whipped along streets, and the official government tourist hotel, at which my stay was mandatory, had electric lights, toilets, and other modern amenities, but none were functional. One hour would have sufficed in Nagqu; instead we spent two days on truck repairs.

A long day's drive west of Nagqu through lush pasturelands over an abominable track took us to the county town of Baingoin. In about 150 miles we saw many pastoralists and much livestock—but not one large wild

PRECEDING PAGES: The mudbrick houses of Shuanghu blend into the somber winter landscape.

ABOVE: Most nomads now have access to information from the outside world through radio.

BELOW: Nomads in Shuanghu play outdoor pool even in subfreezing temperatures.

mammal except a tawny sand fox bolting for its burrow. A few Tibetan gazelles also persisted, I was told. Would the entire Chang Tang be empty like this in the future?

From Baingoin north past Siling Co, the huge Luminous Devil Lake, to Shuanghu is about two hundred miles. We left behind the expanses of alpine meadows with their fine sod layer, characteristic of the eastern edge of the Chang Tang, and entered a more meager habitat, the steppe. Here pastoralists were few, and indeed the region north of Siling Co had been almost unoccupied until the 1960s. Consequently the steppe with its waves of feather grass was still undamaged, one of the greatest and least-known rangelands in the world.

Shuanghu lies at 15,500 feet near the northern edge of this unbroken steppe. It is the usual administrative imposition with a clutter of mudbrick or cement barracks for officials as well as nomads who keep homes here. The town was an ossuary of sheep and yak bones mixed with feces, bits of cloth and plastic, rubber shoe soles, middens of ashes, decomposing dogs, and a glitter of broken glass. (Tibetans are keen customers of beer, and it seems compulsory that bottles be smashed.) Lean dogs prowl the refuse and ravens probe it. Men lounge around, some of them casualties of extinct fashions in bell-bottom trousers and high-heeled shoes. Outdoor pool tables indicate the sport of choice.

ABOVE: When traveling in the Chang Tang, both luck and a measure of cerebral activity are needed to prevent a vehicle from bogging down and delaying us for hours or even days.

LEFT: With the onset of the summer rains, road travel becomes difficult. In the populated southern parts of Tibet, villagers can be hired to help extract a vehicle from a quagmire.

The party secretary of Shuanghu was Suolang Gongbu, a jockey-sized Tibetan wearing a large Mao button, who genially referred to me as the Imperialist American. Every autumn he sent trucks to the far north to shoot wild yaks for winter meat, even though the species is fully protected in China. While we were there he handed several rifles to his staff for a kiang hunt; meat was needed to feed Chinese laborers on a local construction project. When in 1901 Sven Hedin traveled through the Shuanghu region, he found that "yaks and kulans [kiang] were remarkably numerous. Occasionally we counted them by the hundreds." Yaks are gone from the vicinity of Shuanghu, but kiang remain, largely because most Tibetans do not eat them now. In 1993 Suolang Gongbu was named National Wildlife Protection Model by the Tibetan government for his contribution to conservation.

We tore ourselves away from the gross charms of Shuanghu on June 24, too late to observe the chiru's birth season and perhaps too late to escape the heavy summer rains and snows that would make cross-country travel on the sodden ground extremely difficult. However, we had come to study wildlife, and whatever the limitations we wanted to achieve something. I was finally back in the field, my compass pointing north into uninhabited terrain.

At Shuanghu we had been given a guide, Sonanzandu, whom we called Abo, Big Brother. When, no more than twenty miles out of town, we asked him for a possible route north, he said that he had never been there. At least he was a pleasant person and a superbly strong digger when our vehicles bogged down, as they did with frustrating frequency. We tried one route north but the truck subsided in liquid mud hidden beneath an innocuous-looking crust. We attempted another route where hills were lower, but again the truck sank, and it required a full day of exhausting work to extract it. I envied the early explorers with their pack animals. When, within a few miles, the truck once more burrowed in, this time in sand, we decided to continue with only the Land Cruiser, carrying spare gasoline and food for a few days.

We drove sixty miles north as a raven flies through the basin of Linggo Co and along the flanks of glacier-capped Purog Kangri to the shores of a large lake, Dogai Coring. Wildlife was scarce—a few yaks and male chiru—and five days later we rejoined the truck. Perhaps, I suggested, we should try a route a little farther to the west, and Dunzhu, our team's leader, agreed. This year's group from the institute was companionable and remained so in spite of the dispiriting trip so far. Again there was driver Xiong Jigui, five Tibetans, including Abo, as well as Qiu Mingjiang, who had earlier worked with me in other parts of China.

We followed a track west for about eighty miles, past the villages of Garco and Tsasang, and at the tip of the Jangngai Range we turned north once more into a roadless area. The terrain was drier here. We camped by a stream not far from the family of a nomad named Pujung Narla, whose three black tents were tucked into the lee of an ochre slope.

Pujung Narla was small and stocky, in his late fifties, with his hair in the two braids traditional among nomads. He wore a dark cloak of homespun and from his belt hung a pouched *me-cha*, literally fire-steel, decorated with silver and turquoise. With a wide smile, he invited us in for tea. His wife poured boiling tea into a wooden churn that contained salt and butter and mixed these with a plunger. We relaxed by the fire sipping tea from *pobas*, small drinking bowls. A young woman sat in a corner rhythmically shaking an inflated skin bag, turning yogurt to butter. The tent's inner edge was crammed with items of centuries past yet just as useful today: a muzzle loader, sheepskin quilts, wooden milk buckets, ropes of braided yak hair, sacks of barley, pack saddles, wooden chests, and several bricks of butter sewn tightly into sheep stomachs, preserving them for as long as a year. There were modern conveniences too, among them a small-bore rifle, aluminum pots, and a broken radio. A pile of dried yak chips filled one corner. On a box was a private shrine of butter lamps, prayer beads, and a photo of the Panchen Lama,

RIGHT: Pujung Narla, our host on several trips, stands before his tent of woven yak hair holding his muzzle loader. The two prongs on the gun steady the barrel when they have been folded down with the tips resting on the ground.

OVERLEAF: Our overnight camp at seventeen thousand feet looks insignificant in a belligerent landscape of gray gravel and storm clouds.

Tibetan Buddhism's most important incarnation after the Dalai Lama. Pujung Narla told us that he and his extended family are a self-contained unit. Together, they had about a thousand sheep and goats, thirty yaks, and ten horses which grazed in the mountains nearby and seasonally from a satellite camp beyond the next hills. No, he had never been far to the north, not beyond Margog Caka, and he did not know where the female chiru, or *zhi*, as they are called here, go in summer; only a few males remain at this season.

We drove north again through trackless uplands, the hills naked and gray with an icy wind scouring dust from their surface. As Fernand Grenard noted in 1893, it is a land "where nothing passes but the wind, where nothing happens but geological phenomena." Drinkable water was rare in this primeval barrenness; one night we drained fluids from tinned vegetables to cook noodles. A wolf was at a seepage in the fold of a ridge, and we usurped his place to establish a base from which to explore. Taking only the Land Cruiser, we drove northwest to the broad valley of the Tian Shui He, Clear Water River, whose turbid flow starts in the glaciers of the Zangser Kangri, which we had visited the previous year, and ends in a series of lakes. Along the valley's margin, four bull yaks rested out of our sight behind a rise. Startled by our car, three fled but one was rankled and attacked, head high and nostrils flared, his bushy tail swooshing from side to side. Xiong

Jigui tried to accelerate but the car was sluggish in the silt; the galloping yak gained on us until he filled the rear window. Xiong zigzagged the car like a panicked hare, and the yak finally stopped, having thoroughly intimidated us. We camped soon after by a clear pool, a pair of peaceful shelduck as neighbors.

The next day, Abo and I walked up a canyon, a gateway into hills beyond. Tracks of wolf and bear annotated the dry streambed and a snow leopard had left its calling card by scraping the ground with its hindpaws at the base of limestone outcrops. Above, a female blue sheep with a shaky newborn balanced on a cliff ledge. I followed this animal highway until it opened into a hidden sanctuary of rounded hills verdant with grass and herbs. And here were the chiru females that had so far eluded us this trip. It was July 11, the birth season over. But I had found one of their secret retreats. I counted about eight hundred chiru—some slopes rippled with animals—and there were more beyond, farther than we could walk that day and return. Many females were accompanied by their female offspring of the previous year—but not by newborns. Had most females failed to conceive or give birth, as was apparently the case following the blizzard of 1985 in Qinghai? Or had they lost their young in a local disaster, something for which I found no evidence? Perhaps this was not a traditional calving area, merely a good place to halt because further travel was futile. My exhilaration

OPPOSITE: Snow leopards are rare in the reserve, largely because few mountain ranges have enough blue sheep and other prey to support viable cat populations. I photographed this female in the Hindu Kush Mountains of Pakistan.

BELOW: Although I often found snow leopard spoor, such as these tracks, on the Tibetan Plateau, the animal itself remained a phantom.

These hot springs near Rongma in the Yibug Caka Basin have long drawn visitors, from neolithic hunters to present-day pastoralists.

at finding the chiru was tempered by their quiet tragedy.

Rejoining the truck, we drove back to Pujung Narla's place. A creek emerged from the Jangngai Range a few miles away, and at the mouth was a mound from the top of which hot water bubbled. This site, holy to nomads, provided a wide view of the valley and the receding waves of hills beyond. Grazing was good here, attracting chiru and kiang. It was a perfect campsite for pastoralists and hunters. When we had briefly stopped there before, I had noticed a chip of black stone, a piece of basalt, different in color from the other stones, and picked it up. It was a tool from the dim past, a flake with one edge chipped to make a cutting blade, useful in butchering. Now I wanted to search the site more carefully.

Almost immediately, I found another stone tool, probably a hide scraper. I held it in my hand, a trophy of a lost time, making contact over the millennia with someone else who had been here. The scraper was not dead stone: warm hands had made it, scraped flesh and tissue from a hide, perhaps a blue sheep, and discarded it. I tried to resurrect the past, stepping back in time to view the valley with new eyes, those of an early hunter. And having learned to see, I noticed that such ancient handiwork littered the ground around the hot spring, unused fragments chipped off fist-sized chert and basalt pebbles, and broken scrapers and knives, some no doubt once

69

hafted to a handle. At other sites that summer, I had found similar tools and also inch-long cores of chalcedony and jasper from which tiny, sharp slivers had been struck for probable use as arrowheads and fine knives. I later learned that such microblades were once common in Central Asian tool kits; they were developed within the past ten thousand years and persisted until metal became readily available.

To approach and kill a shy creature with such primitive weapons requires patience, ingenuity, and skill. Perhaps hunters hid near a trail, flattened in a shallow hollow—a technique still in use today—until an animal came close enough to pierce with arrow or spear. Perhaps dogs helped them hunt, as described by a nomad to anthropologists Melvyn Goldstein and Cynthia Beall in their excellent book *Nomads of Western Tibet*. "As you will see, as soon as I spot blue sheep on a mountain slope I turn loose my dogs. Their job is to corner one of the *na* [blue sheep] among the crags, and bark loudly to lead me to the spot. . . . Once I get there, I have plenty of time to set up my rifle and shoot. In fact, during the commune period [1970s] when I had no rifle, I climbed above the cornered *na* and heaved down large rocks to kill it."

The most efficient hunting method without guns, past or present, is to use foot traps. Pujang Narla had several such traps—and a bale of hides to prove their effectiveness. The main part of the trap consists of a circle, about six to seven inches in diameter, made from chiru horn or other hard, pliable material covered with coarsely spun yak hair. Short, sharpened prongs of horn or wood point in and down into the circle with the tips almost meeting. The hunter digs an arm-deep hole, places the trap on top, and covers it with grass and soil. A stout rope not only attaches the trap to a stake but also serves as a snare, added insurance should an animal try to pull free. A gazelle or chiru walking down a trail steps into the trap, its leg far in the hole, and cannot retreat without sharp prongs piercing its skin.

Stone tool sites are common in parts of the Chang Tang that today are uninhabited; bands of hunters and later pastoralists (it is unknown when livestock reached the region) had obviously been widespread there at one time, camping along lakeshores, stream banks, and other favorable places. Pollen analysis of lake sediments by Chinese researchers show that the Chang Tang was warmer and wetter five to thirteen thousand years ago than today. Then as now most of the Chang Tang was steppe, but there were also stands of pine and fir as well as thickets of willow and alder, making conditions for these early tenants comparatively pleasant.

In the span of two months I had lived in several realities: as suburban dweller in my Connecticut home, as "foreign expert" making the rounds of government offices in Beijing and Lhasa, as roving naturalist in nomads' tents, and, camped near history, as Stone Age hunter.

A few thousand years ago, when the climate was more benign, nomadic hunters lived in the Chang Tang in areas that are devoid of people today. They camped at lake margins, along freshwater streams, and near hot springs, leaving a litter of stone tools behind. Their tool kits included knives and hide scrapers with carefully flaked edges. Archaeologists estimate that some of these tools may be as much as twenty thousand or thirty thousand years old.

ABOVE: When an animal steps into a trap hidden on a trail, the prongs prevent it from withdrawing its leg.

RIGHT: A nomad carries three leg-hold traps, used to catch chiru, gazelles, and blue sheep.

71

The Spiritual Heart of Tibet

Most *Bodpa*, as the people of Tibet call themselves, are farmers who grow barley and other crops in the south below an elevation of fourteen thousand feet. In the north and northwest, in the harsh, high uplands, pastoralism is the only viable way to subsist. Still, as a Tibetan proverb states, "All roads lead to Lhasa," the holy city of Tibetan Buddhism.

Once known as Rasa, Land of Goats, the town became Lhasa, Seat of the Gods, in the seventh century. It was then that Tibet became a unified empire under King Songtsen Gampo and he made it his capital. The Jokhang temple, "The House of the Master," in the center of Lhasa was built at that time, and pilgrims still flock to this most sacred of temples. The Potala, one of the noblest edifices of the human spirit, was erected on the site of another temple in the mid-seventeenth century by the Fifth Dalai Lama. He was the first to take both religious and secular control of Tibet. Thereafter the Potala was the residence of all Dalai Lamas —a title that means Ocean of Wisdom— until the current Dalai Lama, the fourteenth incarnation, fled to India in 1959. The Potala is nearly 400 feet high and contains, it is said, 999 rooms. The central part is rust-red, and its interior contains many temple rooms and the funerary *chortens*, or stupas, of eight Dalai Lamas, each bejeweled with gold, pearls, and jade.

Pilgrims converge on Lhasa throughout the year but especially in February and March when such important festivals as the Tibetan New Year and the Great Prayer Festival occur. They come by truck and bus and on foot from the Chang Tang and elsewhere to give their votive offerings of butter, *tsamba*, and money. In the shops that ring the Jokhang they buy new clothes, jewelry, household goods, and other items before returning to their distant homes.

Monks at prayer in a temple.

ABOVE: After spending hours or days using colored sand to make an intricate design, monks casually erase it, emphatically illustrating the Buddhist concept of impermanence.

OVERLEAF: Prayer flags, or wind pictures, imprinted with holy images and texts, flutter near the base of the Potala.

A truckload of Chang Tang pilgrims, bundled against the cold, heads toward Lhasa. The people found a female chiru dead beside the road and took it along to eat.

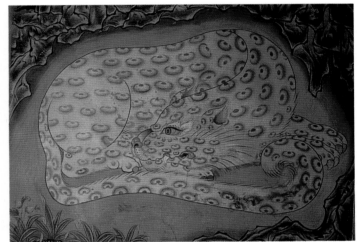

ABOVE: Pilgrims stand in line on the roof of the Potala, waiting to enter a temple. At right, a mural in the Potala includes the image of a snow leopard.

RIGHT: Walls of *mani* stones, inscribed with prayers, are often built near sacred ground. The carved skull of a domestic yak is also on this prayer wall.

Smoke billows before the Jokhang temple
where pilgrims burn incense of juniper
and rhododendron as an offering. On the
roof of the temple is the golden wheel
of knowledge, representing the living
message of Buddhism. A gazelle rests
on each side of the wheel. This symbol
commemorates Buddha's first sermon in
the Park of Gazelles in Benares, India.

ABOVE: A monk counts prayers on his rosary.

OPPOSITE: Intricate carvings and brightly
colored woodwork adorn a courtyard in the
Jokhang temple.

The Dalai Lama belongs to the Gelugpa sect, one of four main sects of Tibetan Buddhism. Another sect follows the Karma Kagyu tradition. Its seat of power since the twelfth century has been the Tsurphu monastery high in a mountain valley near Lhasa. Tsurphu was sacked by Mongols in the 1640s and almost destroyed during the Cultural Revolution of the 1960s, but each time it was rebuilt. The head of the sect is the Gyalwa Karmapa, now in his seventeenth reincarnation. The current Karmapa was born in 1985 and enthroned in 1992.

A festive procession leaves Tsurphu on May 22, 1994, during the first unveiling of a huge new *thangka*, or religious scroll. The previous one had been destroyed a quarter century before during the Cultural Revolution. Several monks carry cylindrical flags, which spread Buddha's truth evenly in all directions.

ABOVE: After the procession, the monks refresh themselves with cups of buttered tea.

LEFT: The *thangka*, measuring 76 × 115 feet and weighing 2000 pounds, was carried to a special place on a hillside and unrolled.

His Holiness Urgyen Trinley Dorje, the Karmapa, looks at an article of mine about the Chang Tang's wildlife in *National Geographic* magazine, a copy of which I presented to him in November 1993. Wildlife was once protected by monks in the vicinity of monasteries, but in recent decades this tradition has all too often lapsed. During my visits to monasteries, I encouraged the renewal of such protection.

November and December 1991

I prefer the tranquility of an
unpeopled world in which to
study animals and roam. But
unfortunately most wildlife in the
Chang Tang shares the steppe of
feather grass with nomads, not
because the animals have an affinity
for people and livestock but
because the grazing is so good
there. The best time to study the
interactions between nomads and
wildlife and census the various
species is in winter, when the chiru
are massed along the northern
fringe of the steppe and it is easy

86

to drive over the dry ground and across frozen streams. We were a small team that winter, just Gu Binyuan and Xiong Jigui from the institute, as well as Dawa, an expansive Tibetan who served as truck driver, cook, and wildlife spotter with cheerful efficiency. And for the first time Ding Li joined us. An English-speaking journalist in his twenties, he was curious about the mysterious Chang Tang and had volunteered to come. He was an excellent field companion, always congenial and ever helpful.

On arrival in Shuanghu it was -25°F and gales blasted across the steppe. The crushing misery of cold would make camping difficult, so we planned our survey in such a way that we could base ourselves at one of three villages —Garco, Tsasang, Rongma—all west of Shuanghu. The track to Garco swings around the northern end of the Amu Range. Dotting the plains and hills were chiru, over a thousand of them of all ages and both sexes. At this season the males are dressed in their finest courtship pelage: ghost-gray and light-tan body with a gleaming white throat and lower neck. Their faces are black, as are broad streaks down the front of each leg. We had probably seen some of these males north of here the previous summer. Back from their secret calving grounds, about half of the adult females had a youngster at heel, reasonably good reproductive success in this population.

Garco was founded in the mid-1970s when thirty-six families moved there from the vicinity of Xianza, a twenty-day walk to the south, settling on pasturelands that were then uninhabited. Today it consists of a cluster of mudbrick quarters tucked against low hills with a view of Chargamu Co and the Amu Range beyond. A small forest of twenty-four windmills grows above the village roofs, designed for generating electricity, but none are functioning. A large dish antenna eyes the sky, but it too is a monument to failed ambition.

The party secretary since the village's founding has been Bema, a tall autocrat who makes all decisions for the community. He decides who will herd livestock, build houses, slaughter animals, and sew garments, and he gives permission for marriages and divorces. For a modest fee, Bema allowed us to occupy a hut. It was just large enough for our sleeping bags and a metal stove that emitted bursts of smoke with every gust of wind. We had a choice of two fuels: yak chips, which burn hot but fast, and sheep and goat pellets, which are merely warm but last a long time. Either way the chill seeped into us and only our sleeping bags brought real warmth. The stars were closer and brighter than I had ever seen, and the nights were calm but also long. During the twelve to thirteen hours of enforced idleness in a sleeping bag, ordinary matters such as the long cold journey to the outhouse intruded at the most inconvenient times. The village did not stir until 9 AM, when a weak sun relieved the frigid night. Women carried buckets of ashes to dump at the village's edge, and ravens arrived from a cliff roost to sift

PRECEDING PAGES: A herd of kiang drums over the brittle grasslands of winter. Kiang concentrate on good pastures in that season, with more than two hundred together at times.

through garbage. Xiong Jigui was forced to heat the engine block with a blow torch to induce the car to start.

For this trip we had set ourselves the ambitious task of counting chiru, kiang, gazelles, and yaks within a 6700-square mile rectangle of steppe and mountains. Day after day we crossed plains and basins, traced the flow of valleys up and down and over passes, and scanned slopes, checking and counting until we had covered most of the area. Officials and nomads told us repeatedly of the thousands, the millions, the inexhaustible numbers of animals that exist here and to the north. A thousand chiru concentrated like ants on a hill or a herd of a hundred, two hundred, kiang drumming across the sun-burned steppe, hooves trailing feathers of dust, the whole landscape seemingly in motion, are spectacles of overflowing abundance. But casual observers forget that many square miles have little or no wildlife. In our survey area we counted 3900 chiru, 1224 kiang, 352 gazelles, and a mere 13 yaks. These were of course minimum figures and did not include blue sheep and the few argalis. Even so, the area averaged no more than one animal per square mile. Yet the steppe between Shuanghu in the east and Rongma in the west was generally considered to be one of the best places for wildlife in the Chang Tang.

When we arrived at Rongma, in the basin of Yibug Caka, the village leader, So Da, told us that a bear, a large male, had been killed at a nomad's tent two days before. Did we want to see him? Fieldwork offers unpredictable opportunities; we visited the site immediately. The bear's hide was stretched out to dry by the tent. Nearby was the frozen body of a black dog. An old woman had been home alone when the bear came. As the bear killed the dog, the woman ran away, and the bear then entered her tent and ate a leg of mutton. Later that day the woman's son tracked the bear and shot him less than a mile from the tent. I examined the carcass; his canines were mere stumps, and his body was emaciated, wholly depleted of fat. Close to starvation, he had left his winter den to find food. Xiong Jigui severed one of the bear's legs, planning to gain strength by eating it.

Two chiru males spar while a third observes the encounter. Their lance-like horns can inflict such serious injuries that the animals tend to avoid conflict.

That day Party Secretary Min Jia, a high prefecture official from Nagqu, arrived in Rongma on tour. I met him after dinner to discuss wildlife issues. An affable Tibetan of middle age, he told me: "Hunting has been banned. There is no hunting now." A Tibetan gazelle, freshly shot, was in the back of his Land Cruiser.

Two days later, high in the hills above Rongma, we came upon a lone tent with three men; blood-red chiru carcasses were stacked like cordwood by the tent and next to them were severed chiru heads. These men, together with three other teams, had left Gerze by yak caravan twenty-nine days before and traveled over 130 miles to hunt chiru here with trap and rifle. They had killed twenty-two of the animals at this location during the past ten days. The hides were neatly folded in a pile in the back of the tent. The meat would be eaten and the hides and horns sold. Chiru horns are valued in traditional medicines—Tibetans even sell them on the streets in Beijing—and they have other uses as well. The two-pronged fork used to hold a muzzle loader steady while aiming is often made of chiru horns, as are tent stakes and whip handles that are said to keep a horse from tiring.

Through various encounters, such as with this hunter's camp near Rongma, I became aware that here in the Chang Tang, in one of the most isolated corners of the earth, a species was quietly moving toward the shadows of extinction. Everyone from nomad and trader

to officials at various levels was involved in the illicit but lucrative business of dealing in chiru wool, even though the species is completely protected in China and considered to be endangered by international convention. Police and military posts loaned high-powered rifles to nomads in exchange for chiru hides. County officials sent out trucks to kill chiru by the hundreds. The pace and scale of the slaughter was such that within a few years it would reduce the last great herds to tragic remnants. In Baingoin, for instance, I was told that the county leader organized the killing of at least a thousand chiru a year (he was later arrested), and the military post there did so much illegal hunting that a special police and military force was sent to stop it. Most such hunting was done in winter when vehicles can traverse the Chang Tang with ease, chiru are accessible, and meat does not spoil.

Why was there such an intensive commercial slaughter of chiru? Because chiru wool is the finest in the world. *Shahtoosh*, the King of Wool. The wool is woven into scarves and shawls that serve as luxury items and status symbols for the wealthy, the "ultimate emblem of New Age snobbery," as one newspaper article called it. Scarves and shawls sell for $1000–$2000 and up, the larger ones for as much as $8000, in India, Europe, Japan, and North America.

Traders, often Tibetans from Kham in the east, buy the chiru hides, pluck the wool, stuff it into bags, and then smuggle it out of

OPPOSITE: A mother and son sit by the hide of a Tibetan brown bear. The animal entered their tent in search of food.

A hunter checks his trapline.

Whatever happiness is in the world
Has all arisen from a wish for the
Welfare of other beings.
Whatever misery there is has arisen
From indulging in selfishness.

Buddhist precept

A poacher stands in camp by his larder of frozen chiru carcasses and severed chiru heads. The meat is usually eaten by the nomads, the horns are sold to be ground into medicines, and the high-priced hides are passed on to wool dealers. The wooden pack frames are used on yaks for carrying loads.

After buying chiru hides from the nomads, traders from eastern Tibet pluck the wool for illegal export to India.

Tibet by various routes. One such route goes west into the Ladakh area of India, another to Lhasa and then by highway to Nepal, and a third to the town of Burang, south of holy Mount Kailas, and from there into northwest Nepal and on to India. Whatever the route, all wool is destined for Kashmir, because only the weavers there have the skill to handle the extremely fine fibers. By the time the wool has made the long journey it is worth over $600 a pound. To stimulate the sale of *shahtoosh* and make it acceptable to buyers who are ecologically aware, Kashmiri dealers promote a fantasy: diligent shepherds, they say, only pick up shed wool benignly from bushes and rocks where animals have rubbed themselves.

A small *shahtoosh* trade had for centuries been conducted between Tibet and Kashmir. Among wealthy Indians a shawl was traditionally a part of the dowry, the so-called ring shawl so fine that it will easily pass through a wedding ring. "It was like having a sable coat," an Indian woman once told me. However, an unrestrained slaughter of chiru began in the mid-1980s when Western nations discovered *shahtoosh* and used it to make a fashion statement.

In 1991 the Tibet Forest Bureau began to suppress this wool trade, and it has since then confiscated thousands of hides from nomads and dealers. Officials in India estimated that more than 4400 pounds of chiru wool entered the country in 1992, the product of about thirteen thousand chiru. One consignment seized by customs in Delhi in May 1993 weighed 235 pounds. With Tibet disrupting the chiru trade, Chinese hunters became active in Qinghai and Xinjiang. In April 1993, near the Arjin Shan Reserve, a routine check of four trucks in a seventeen-truck convoy headed for Lhasa revealed 674 chiru hides, according to Howman Wong, a Hong Kong–based photographer. I had come to study chiru because I found the species intriguing. But now I observed them with foreboding, knowing that this was their final refuge and hoping that any insights would not merely serve as an obituary.

That winter of 1991 we had come to census wildlife, but I also had another agenda, one strictly devoted to chiru. I have avoided referring to the animal as Tibetan antelope, its more usual designation, because the word "antelope" hides its true antecedents. During the 1930s a paleontologist, G. E. Pilgrim, looked at chiru skulls and decided that the animal is not an antelope but a caprid, a member of the subfamily that includes the sheep and goats. Yet chiru look like antelopes, with their lithe beauty and the male's long, slender horns. I wondered if behavior could help elucidate the chiru's taxonomic position, and the best time to observe behavior is during the rut when animals have congregated and interact.

The rut had begun by mid-December. Chiru aggregated at certain sites, and during our survey we found thirteen such areas, each with at least 100 animals. One courtship arena was in an ancient dry lake bed near Tsasang, a village of seventeen families. I observed the animals there for several days, usually by myself, but at times accompanied by Ding Li.

The days were warm, usually around 0°F, the sky clear, and there were even periods when the wind relaxed. I sat on an old beach line with the chiru below. A number of males stood alone and erect, well spaced, advertising themselves to the females that casually drifted over the area in small herds. At first I thought that the males might be territorial, but I soon noted that they readily left a site. A male sometimes chased another at full tilt for half a mile or more without returning. Sometimes males sparred with locked horns, pushing and twisting, and according to Cecil Rawling, who observed chiru in the early 1900s, they may jab with their spear-like horns until "blood flows freely."

If females come into a male's temporary domain, he tries to detain them, prancing around them with muzzle raised to reveal his white throat. Occasionally he roars with head lowered, the peculiar walnut-sized sac on each nostril apparently acting as a resonator, and he raises his tail, the long white hairs waving in the wind like a prayer flag. The females usually walk or trot off, ignoring his exhibition, and he occasionally tags along. But if a female bolts, enticing him, he races after her, the two skimming the plains with a glorious burst of energy. When receptive, the female

ABOVE: Some nomads have access to high-powered rifles, as these cartridge cases attest. The man's *chuba* is trimmed with otter fur.

RIGHT: Chiru horns are offered for sale near the Jokhang temple in Lhasa, together with sheep and domestic yak skulls and gold-colored prayer wheels.

OPPOSITE: A trader in a Lhasa stall sells leopard, tiger, and otter skins, among other items. The leopard and tiger skins may have originated in the forested parts of southeast Tibet or been imported from Nepal or India.

stops to permit his approach. Gingerly he comes close, body held low and muzzle stretched forward, afraid to spook her. Finally he advances in a high-stepping gait and with a stiff foreleg kicks her gently on the thigh. Balanced bolt upright on his hindlegs he then tries to mount, barely touching her.

Many of the male's dominance and courtship rituals are widespread among ruminants. The male's roaring display resembles one I had seen in African impala. The gentle foreleg kick is present in caprids and many antelopes although absent in some, such as the impala. Various species mount in an upright posture, but most lean heavily on the female and clasp her. The small dik-dik antelope and its relatives, as well as the gazelles, differ from other antelopes in that they barely touch the female while mounting, the same pattern as seen in chiru. Male chiru may also stand erect with legs stiffly forward and back to urinate, and then on rare occasions they squat to defecate at the same spot, a striking display which is found in gazelles, impala, and pronghorn. In brief, no single behavior links the chiru unquestionably to any particular antelope. Its closest behavioral affinity appears to be with the gazelles and perhaps also the impala, a species of ancient lineage of which it is the sole representative.

George Amato of the Wildlife Conservation Society analyzed the chiru's mitochondrial DNA and confirmed Pilgrim's morphological work: the chiru is indeed not an antelope but a caprid. Yet it is not *just* a caprid, because it retains certain physical and behavioral traits from a remote common ancestor among the antelopes. The antelopes, including the gazelles, split from the caprids during the Miocene, when the Tibetan Plateau reached close to its present height, some eight million years ago. This provided a new and unique habitat for several caprids that no doubt evolved there, the blue sheep (actually most closely related to goats), Tibetan argali sheep, and chiru. Each adapted to a certain type of terrain: blue sheep to the vicinity of cliffs, argalis to high rolling hills, and chiru to plains. The Tibetan gazelle, kiang, and possibly wild yak also evolved on the plateau.

Although I became a naturalist to satisfy my curiosity and for the pleasure of new insights, such as this glimpse into the chiru's past, I also seek emotional involvement with the animals themselves. My days with chiru on this high and windy plain provided both. Once I walked among the chiru and sat down immobile, an inanimate hump. The animals soon ignored me. A wolf strolled along a distant cutbank. Even a nomad's tent huddled by a far ridge was part of this landscape. All around me chiru males bellowed their challenges and pursued each other into the blinding light of the horizon; all around me chiru danced on the tawny grass in their ritual of renewal. I sat at the center of this consecrated space, quietly celebrating the harmonious balance of a fleeting moment.

OPPOSITE: Chiru males are often alone during the rut, watching and waiting for females.

June and July 1992

During the summer of 1897, Captain H. Deasy was exploring in northwest Tibet when, north of the Aru Basin, he came upon a great plain covered with huge chiru herds. He named the area Antelope Plain. Six years later, another British officer, Captain Cecil Rawling, found "thousands upon thousands" of chiru there in July. I surmised that the Antelope Plain must be one of the chiru's traditional calving grounds. Fortunately the Tibet Plateau Institute and the Tibet Forest Bureau agreed to a joint trip with Kay and me to that area. Gu Binyuan and Chi Doa were the leaders, as in 1990, and Ding Li again volunteered to come.

From Lhasa to Shiquanhe is a six-day drive. A drab town of dispiriting cement buildings, Shiquanhe is the administrative center for western Tibet; on a nearby hillside is the slogan, made of large white pebbles, "Long live Chairman Mao." A major road link connecting Shiquanhe to Xinjiang provides melons, apples, and other produce in season, as well as gasoline. Only here in all of western Tibet could we obtain the fifteen barrels of gasoline we needed.

At a rebuilt temple in Rutog, students read from typical loose-leaf religious texts. Tibet has the highest illiteracy rate in China: 44 percent of people over the age of fifteen cannot read or write.

PRECEDING PAGE: A male lynx rests on a rocky hill. Though nowhere common, lynx remain widespread in Tibet, and their hides are often seen in markets. They prey on a variety of small mammals and also kill chiru and sheep on occasion.

We drove north to Rutog, which I had first visited in 1988. The old village clusters around the base of a hill whose summit is crowned by the ruin of a monastery that appears to have stood there for centuries. However, these remnants of gray towers and walls were not a medieval memory battered by time and elements, but by the Cultural Revolution of the late 1960s. Although the ruin resonates with sadness, a small temple in it has been rebuilt and there boys were at school, reading Tibetan from loose-leaf texts. Two elderly women greeted us with the old Tibetan custom of sticking out their tongues. Our road north traced the fjord-like Panggong Co which extends for nearly a hundred miles into India. In passing I did a little bird watching—gray herons, bar-headed geese, common mergansers, common pochard, and redshanks, among others. We

spent a night at Domar, a military post among sere mountains with a small marsh that a pair of black-necked cranes claimed as their summer home. At the edge of Domar is a Tibetan motel and trading post. That evening a truck arrived from the vicinity of the Aru Basin. The driver told us that many pregnant chiru were still migrating north-ward; so this year we would not be too late. His truck contained the dried hide of a brown bear and three male chiru he had shot on the way to Domar, planning to sell them here.

At Lungma Co, 1300 miles from Lhasa, we turned off the highway and headed east toward Antelope Plain and into bitter wind and black cloud; that night snow swept over our tents. To my surprise, on crossing a small range the next day we met several nomads. They told us that grazing is poor here and that the country is completely uninhabited beyond Bangdag Co just to the east. Farther on the truck sank deep into mud, and it took a day of toil to release it: jack up one wheel, push rocks into the mud beneath it, jack up the other wheels, then the first again, raising the heavy load inch by inch, and finally place some boards by the wheels with the hope that, together with a pull from the Land Cruiser, the truck will escape the morass. That evening we reached Puer Co, its surface roiled by wind. Ahead was Toze Kangri, 20,800 feet high, its smooth glacial summit adding an icy touch to the scene. We were at the edge of Antelope Plain, and it was only June 6.

We had seen little wildlife so far—a few kiang, male chiru, and yaks, all that the meager habitat can support. The great steppe was to the south. This was desert, a bleak high ground, most of it 16,500 feet and higher, where grasses and sedges grew only in patches and where large tracts were devoid of vegetation except for occasional gray-leafed *Ceratoides* shrubs partially buried in silt. Spring had not yet come, the grasses yellow without even a hint of green. Yue Ya Hu, a small lake we passed the next day, remained frozen except for leads along the shore. There we saw several pregnant chiru and with great anticipation we entered Antelope Plain.

But it was empty. The vast gray expanse was empty and absolutely still except for a few stray chiru which seemed absorbed by the immense landscape. Where were the great herds?

We drove toward some low hills to find a place to camp and selected the banks of a glacial stream that flowed from Toze Kangri. Or, rather, the site selected us when the truck bogged down there. The following ten days

On every trip our heavily loaded truck sank into mud or sand many times. Here, from front to back, Wen Bin, Danzhen, Dawa, and Ding Li try to extricate it.

were memorable for their misery. Wind and snow lashed camp almost nightly, and Kay and I knew that each tomorrow we would most likely rue yet another lost day. Nothing ever seemed gentle here. Every morning I looked out into a trackless white void. The thermometer registered 20°F, and with my hands I raked a foot of snow from around the base of the tent. Spring in the Chang Tang. The sun would soon melt most of the night's snow but then leave the ground sodden, the soil remaining undrained because of permafrost only two to three feet below the surface. We tried to find the chiru, surveying east and north to two remote lakes, Bairab Co and Jianshui Hu, the wheels of the Land Cruiser churning deep grooves in the terrain and using precious gasoline. But the chiru had vanished.

All too often we were bound to camp by weather and fuel shortage, and then I took long walks. To the southwest was Toze Kangri and just to the north another glacier peak, both suspended above the earth, carried by clouds. Striding into this dense silence, into this infinite space with no sign of life other than the scribbles of pika tracks in the snow connecting burrow to burrow, I was immersed in a landscape of desolation, emptiness, and potential peril. But these characteristics are part of what makes this wilderness so exceptional. I am most comfortable at the edge of existence in a remote place such as this; perhaps it suits my temperament, reflecting

Almost from my feet away to the north and east, as far as the eye could reach, were thousands upon thousands of doe antelope with their young. The mothers were mostly feeding, while the young ones were either lying down and resting, or being urged on by their mothers. All had their heads turned towards the west, and were travelling slowly in that direction, presumably in search of the fresh young grass springing up in the high western tablelands.

Everyone in camp turned out to see this beautiful sight, and tried, with varying results, to estimate the number of animals in view. This was found very difficult, however, more particularly as we could see in the extreme distance a continuous stream of fresh herds steadily approaching; there could not have been less than 15,000 or 20,000 visible at one time.

—Captain C. Rawling
The Great Plateau, 1905

I am "chasing after the vestiges of a vanished reality,"
as Claude Lévi-Strauss phrased it, mourning the
great herds that once were. Photo by Kay Schaller

TOP: Dawa, "Moon" in Tibetan, heats tea water with a blowtorch during our futile search for the chiru's calving grounds on the Antelope Plain.

ABOVE: During days in camp when travel was not possible, the team members amused themselves by playing cards, talking, and sleeping, and one day Dawa and Wen Bin built a snowman.

RIGHT: Kay heads toward the cook tent for breakfast after another June night of snow.

an inner landscape, a certain taciturn spirit, or perhaps it indicates a quest for something clear-cut and explicit. Certainly some of the expeditions in the past found little pleasure in the Chang Tang. Gabriel Bonvalot wrote of "the solitude being deeper and weighing heavier than ever," and Fernand Grenard noted that "our men, terrified at this endless mountain desert, were seized with an ardent longing to escape from it, to see something different." They saw in the Chang Tang a sprawling purgatory they had to cross for a distant goal, that of Lhasa; I wanted to escape into it, fearful that the terrible weather would deprive me of time here. A sense of place is based less on reality than on what it symbolizes.

On rare occasions I met a bull yak on my walks, he and I the only features in this expanse that did not radiate light. On detecting me, the bull would trot off with resignation, moving on and on, his blue tongue hanging out from the exertion, continuing until he dwindled to a speck against the glare even in my scope, and finally vanishing as if stepping over the rim of the earth.

Kay and I had a golden tent that was visible from afar. As I trudged home it gave me a perspective of size and distance in this limitless land. It was also a sunny island of human warmth. On returning I gratefully sipped hot tea from the thermos that Kay handed me.

These desert steppes represent life at the limit for most species. I saw only seventy-three yaks in about three thousand square miles; kiang were rare, chiru seasonal, gazelles absent. Pikas supported a few bears. One day we came upon a rock pinnacle with two half-fledged saker falcon young in a niche. I almost overlooked a lynx resting casually on the cliff, his coat blending into the rock. Apparently he had never seen humans before and thought us inconsequential; there was not even fire in his eyes as he gazed upon us. He presumably subsisted on the few woolly hares in the area. There was so little vegetation that upland hawks could not obtain enough material to build their eyries and supplemented the usual sticks with old chiru horns.

With existence here so marginal, why do female chiru vacate the fine steppe in the south, just as it is green with high-quality forage? They come to this naked land with its sparse winter-dry grazing when they are most in need of nutritious food—during late gestation and early lactation, two periods of great energy drain. Perhaps certain plants rich in some nutrient such as phosphorus and calcium, which are needed for growth, occur here. Or possibly by calving together during a brief period in a bleak place they reduce predation on helpless newborns; limited by lack of prey, few wolves can live here permanently, and the packs in the south cannot commute north as long as they have small pups. After giving birth, chiru immediately head south again on another tiring trek. In 1990 they had reached the Aru Basin by early August. Why do the chiru

We found the mummified body of a bull yak, and Dawa playfully bulldogs it.

migrate? Once more an answer might elude me.

On June 16 we drove west to Yue Ya Hu, close to Toze Kangri, to establish a new camp. Fortunately the truck got stuck again, for while we were digging it out about 350 chiru females passed us, intently heading northeast. Here was the migration route! The herds funneled out of one valley, passed the western spurs of Toze Kangri, crossed a flat, and then vanished high among the foothills of an unnamed glacier peak. At least two thousand females hurried past camp in four days, and then numbers dropped sharply, the migration essentially over. We moved camp again, this time close to the glacier peak. The night snows continued, making vehicle travel ever more difficult. Once I slowly followed a herd of fifty-eight females over the hills for eight miles on foot and watched as they headed across a plain toward a range beyond. That day the Tibetans Wen Bin and Dawa also searched the hills. They met three wolves on a freshly killed female and had an inadvertent meeting with a short-tempered bear which charged them. And they saw several lone female chiru, each with a newborn. Such lagging females had apparently misjudged their timing and had given birth en route. Although Wen Bin was our cook and Dawa the truck driver, they entered into the spirit of our conservation work more than most of those on our journeys. *Om mani padme hum,* Hail oh jewel in the lotus, is the Tibetan invocation for the salvation of all living crea-

tures. I had brought several small prayer flags from Lhasa, and Wen Bin built a cairn on a nearby hill and draped it with these flags, a visual entreaty for good luck and protection of wildlife here.

We split up. I left with one team for the north on a day adrift in mist and snow. When the clouds lifted, as they usually did by late morning, we saw ahead a bald, low range strewn with black volcanic boulders and pimpled with several volcanic cones. At the foot of this range was a red-rock hillock, a stream, and a wolf latrine; chiru droppings pebbled a nearby slope. It was a good spot for our tents.

On a following day, Dawa and I went north into the hills in search of the chiru. Above us, snow-filled ravines descended the slope in graceful curves resembling white ceremonial scarves, or *katas*. We climbed, following braided chiru tracks. Ridge followed ridge and still the crest was beyond, but then suddenly the terrain dropped away; my altimeter read 17,200 feet. Below was a huge basin divided into two arms. Giant peaks of the Kunlun Shan bordered the arm most distant from us and sent glaciers down to the basin floor. Across from us and dividing the arms were three massive volcanoes, their tops blown off and covered with snow and ice. In the basin were two lakes connected by a stream: a small lake sheathed in ice and a much larger lake extending toward the northeast. At least five small volcanic cones and

Black-necked cranes nest in marshes of the southern
Chang Tang, not within the reserve. Tibetans revere
cranes, with the result that the birds have little fear of
people. At least 5500 of these cranes exist. They spend
the summer in the high marshlands and descend for the
winter to southern Tibet, Yunnan, and Bhutan.

LEFT: The only reptile in the reserve is a small lizard, *Phrynocephalus theobaldi*, which may be found as high as seventeen thousand feet, where it lives on spiders and insects.

BELOW LEFT: Tibetan sand grouse are pigeon-sized birds with a light buff plumage and yellow cheeks and throat. Small flocks streak across the sky over even the highest and most desolate plains. A sand grouse nest consists of a bare, shallow cup in the soil, perhaps lined with a few pebbles, and contains two or three large, speckled eggs from which entrancing downy chicks hatch.

A Tibetan woolly hare huddles by some lava boulders in an attempt to remain inconspicuous. The species is endemic to the Tibetan Plateau, where it is preyed upon by lynx, wolf, and other predators.

Wolves are usually encountered singly or in twos. Intensely disliked by nomads—and practically everyone else—wolves are likely to survive only in those parts of the Chang Tang that are uninhabited by people.

lava fields were along the eastern margin of the large lake, which Chinese maps aptly call Heishi Beihu, Blackrock Northlake. I viewed the topography with special interest. The chiru had vanished here, and, to my knowledge, no other Westerner had ever viewed this imposing scene, one of the most remote and untrodden spots on earth. Deasy, Rawling, Wellby, and Hedin had all bypassed this basin.

But my concern was with chiru, not geography. Dawa and I scanned the basin from end to end, and again. It seemed devoid of life. Dead. The hills beyond the basin were relatively low, affording an easy pass into Xinjiang, and the chiru must have gone that way. We descended the escarpment, still following tracks, knowing the gesture was futile but unwilling to admit it. The basin floor was a desolation of muddy frost heaves and barren soil with only occasional patches of vegetation. In three hours of walking we saw just six chiru, one a newborn. The others had already passed through, moving steadily toward their traditional and mysterious goal, too far for us to follow with our limited gasoline supply. As we prepared to leave for the Aru Basin, there to await the return migration, Chi Doa said to me, "Perhaps we were fated not to discover where the chiru go."

There is a Tibetan proverb that says "the goal will not be reached if the right distance is not traveled." Clearly I had not traveled far enough; I would try another year.

July and August 1992

Even before we reached it, I knew that the Aru Basin had changed. Two years earlier we had had to search for a route over the Aru Range; this year a well-worn vehicle track led us through the pass. From our old campsite I saw not wildlife but more than a thousand domestic sheep. A truck passed, going north on a beaten track, and the next day two more followed, all laden high with nomads' possessions. It was the new nomadism, if you could afford it. Others still transported their belongings in a traditional manner.

ABOVE: Tied side by side in two lines, goats wait to be milked. The woman's milk pail is a wild yak horn. Goats are milked twice daily in summer, but the animals produce little in winter.

PRECEDING PAGES: Chiru migrate past Luotuo Hu, Camel Lake, toward the Aru Range, a vision of pure delight.

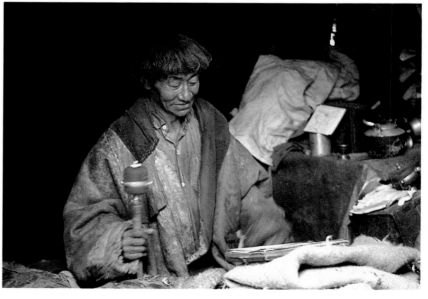

A nomad reads from a religious text and at the same time spins his prayer wheel. Inside the wheel is a printed prayer. Every revolution of the wheel is the equivalent of reciting the prayer once.

Two men carrying muzzle loaders came by, driving a herd of yaks with swaying loads—tents and tent poles, bundles and sacks, children, pots, and newborn lambs—and behind them were two women driving sheep, and a swarm of dogs. They said that about fifteen families had moved into the basin, most of them temporarily, because heavy snows this year made grazing in the mountains difficult.

At the northern end of Memar Co, where the wolves had denned, were five nomad families, their black tents squatting like tarantulas among the low hills. We visited Chida, the headman of this small cluster of people. His hair was close-cropped and gray and he had a quiet dignity. After we were seated in his tent, I gave Chida a card, as I do all nomads. One side has a drawing of Milarepa, Tibet's most famous saint and poet, amid peaceful animals and a kneeling hunter who has forever laid down his arms—a sword, bow, and quiver of arrows; the other side quotes Buddha, in Tibetan script, stating that one should neither kill nor cause to kill. Chida reverently touched the edge of the card to his forehead and placed it on his shrine next to a photo of the Dalai Lama. Most Tibetans are devout Buddhists and in principle adhere to one of Buddha's principal tenets: "Kindness to all living things is the true religion."

Tibetans usually move leisurely but they always seem busy with some task. As we began our talk with Chida, his wife sat by the fire making yarn by twirling a hand spindle.

Just outside the tent two women milked about forty goats tied in two tight rows, heads facing inward. Chida told us, with Dawa as translator, that he was sixty-eight years old, born in a valley just to the west, and that his father and grandfather had lived here. The five families included about forty people, among them eighteen children, none of whom went to school. Together the five families had about six hundred sheep and forty-five yaks.

These families were obviously poor, with too few livestock to sustain so many people. After all, every person needs some four sheep as food per year, and nomads prefer not to slaughter more than about 10 percent of their flocks annually. In the past Chida had brought livestock into the Aru Basin for only two to three months in summer. But last year the families had settled here permanently. Chida admitted that he had moved into the Aru Basin for one purpose only: to hunt chiru. Their meat preserved the lives of his sheep whose fleece brought much-needed cash, and from the sale of chiru hides the family had made enough money to buy a truck. But a truck requires expensive maintenance and fuel. Indeed, it had left the previous day with about fifty chiru hides to trade for gasoline.

Melvyn Goldstein and Cynthia Beall wrote in 1990 that among nomads, "hunting wild animals and butchering livestock are again taking on the stigma they had in traditional society." I could sense such reluctance toward hunting on Chida's part. But he had

TOP: A snowstorm prevented a Hume's ground jay from finding insects to eat, and it ventured to a nomad's tent where a frozen sheep carcass provided bits of meat and fat.

ABOVE: Two juvenile black-lipped pikas touch noses in greeting at a burrow entrance. These plains-living pikas are an important component of the food chain in that many predators, from saker falcons to foxes and bears, depend on them. Pikas live in families consisting of an adult male and female with their five to ten juveniles from at least two litters.

had to put compassion and regret aside and chose stigma over minimal subsistence. I had a measure of sympathy for his predicament. Pastoralists have traditionally hunted for subsistence, though not as a large-scale commercial venture. In 1906, for example, Sven Hedin came upon a tent inhabited by a woman and three children. "She had arrived from Gertse [Gerze] 17 days before with her two husbands, who had returned to Gertse after they had filled her tent for her with wild-ass meat. She owned a few yaks and small flock of sheep and would live for the next three months on game—yaks, kiangs, and antelopes."

Chida also pointed out that since everyone else was killing the wild animals, he might as well too. Twice the previous winter Tibetan officials from Gerze had come to the Aru Basin to hunt yaks and chiru with modern weapons. "If the officials obey the law and stop hunting, we will too," he said.

We needed meat, and Chida agreed to sell us a ram, to be picked up two days later. When we returned, the sheep was tied to a post. Chida bound its feet and laid it on its side. He poured water into the sheep's mouth from a small blue teapot. If it swallowed the water then it was resigned to death; it swallowed. He then lashed its muzzle closed with a thong, cutting off air to nose and mouth. As the sheep quietly died, Chida said a prayer to the animal's spirit while he fingered his rosary and spun a prayer wheel.

It was not long from death to dinner. We were hungry. And we had moved camp to Memar Co, a few miles south of Chida's encampment, because disturbance from the nomads at Aru Co was so great that most wildlife had moved away. Our tents were tucked against a bluff by a stream. Judging by its droppings, a brown bear had occasionally rested on that bluff, with a superb view of the basin.

Kay and I enjoyed this camp and its neighbors. By a grass tuft, a horned lark had a nest with two dark-splotched eggs; night snows often covered the nest except for a small hole, and peering down I would meet the bright gaze of the lark looking up from its igloo. A Hume's ground jay pair had selected an abandoned pika burrow as a nest site. Sparrow-sized with tan plumage and curved bill, the sprightly jays were continually busy, darting in and out of the hole feeding nestlings. Kay, who regularly watched their comings and goings, told me one evening: "Three adults have been bringing insects all day." This nest had not just a pair of adults, but also a helper, probably a fledgling from the previous year. Pikas scurried near our tents, most of them youngsters. On meeting they greeted nose to nose and occasionally reared up to box each other, whether in play or annoyance was not always clear. An infant hare had also chosen a pika burrow as a home. Kay first found it, still as a rock and ears tucked in, by its burrow absorbing the sun's warmth like a tranquil cat. We added it to our circle of local friends.

Late July is the birth season of kiang and

Tibetan gazelles. Unlike kiang foals, which totter at their mother's side within hours after birth, newborn gazelles hide themselves for two to three weeks until they are strong and fleet. One day, not far from camp, a female gazelle was reluctant to flee. She walked stiffly and at times bounced into the air in a series of leaps that made her conspicuous. Surely her young was hidden nearby. I finally found it lying motionless, its neck stretched along the ground. With eyes wide and glistening it watched me approach to within five feet—a deadly predator about to pounce—yet its instincts told it to remain absolutely still. I retreated, watched by an anxious mother a hundred yards away.

Dawa and Wen Bin had also roamed, and on their return they told me of a large yak herd. I was delighted with the news, because yaks were only half as abundant in the basin this year as in 1990; I had hoped they had moved away and had not been killed. The next morning the basin was under a lid of cloud and Memar Co shone like molten lead. We searched for the yaks and found a herd of twenty-nine. Sighting us, they immediately fled, climbing into the mountains, up into the snow, plowing onward to the top of a ridge. Ahead, around a curve of the hills, were another 150 or so yaks on the slopes, and forty more on the plains, placidly grazing.

Suddenly the forty yaks bunched and bolted. Five lanky wolves pursued the herd, surging around and through it. After a head-long rush the yaks halted and stood indecisively. On occasion a wolf swept close past an animal as if testing it, or a yak made a token rush with lowered horns. I suspected that the wolves were in search of a calf, but, seeing none, they did not press their attack. The wolves stood together to one side of the herd; one wolf wagged its tail. A sixth wolf appeared on a rise and the others loped toward it.

I counted a total of 236 yaks on these slopes, of which only three were young of the year. An adult female raises at most one offspring every two years. Since young are generally born in late May and June, I would expect about 10 to 15 percent of the population to consist of young at this time of year. Yet the actual figure was 1 percent, far too few to sustain the population. The almost complete absence of one-year-olds indicated that reproductive success in 1991 had been just as dismal. Why? Wolves no doubt killed some young, but not all. Perhaps livestock had introduced a disease such as brucellosis that can cause spontaneous abortion.

On July 28 a herd of chiru females appeared at the northern end of Aru Basin, the vanguard of the return migration. Two days later we stood high on the rim of the basin looking north into the desert steppe. To our left rose the Aru Range in crystalline aloofness and below among austere hills was Luotuo Hu, Camel Lake, its turquoise waters a reflection of the sky. Two ravens performed aerial antics. No scene in the Chang Tang has so imprinted itself on my memory. With its ecological wholeness, stark beauty, and sense of unfettered freedom, it is a place where mind and body can travel, where one's soul can dance. It is the essence of the Chang Tang.

When across the valley a hill appeared to

A newborn Tibetan gazelle crouches motionless, an innate response designed to avoid detection by predators.

ABOVE: When a chiru herd halts briefly during its migratory trek, the young, only a month old, rest and suckle.

RIGHT: Kay counts chiru from the rim of the Aru Basin as they migrate south from the calving grounds.

be in motion, I thought of heat waves and high-altitude hallucinations, but binoculars revealed waves of chiru, hundreds upon hundreds, on the slopes and on the flats flowing out of a valley from the northeast. I tried to count the animals and at the same time marveled at this Pleistocene vision. Elated beyond measure, I returned to camp, eager to take Kay to view this pastoral delight the next day.

The chiru did not migrate south through the Aru Basin, a logical and easy route, but westward across a pass of the Aru Range into the basin of Lumajangdong Co and from there southward. Nomads told us that the animals also bypassed the Aru Basin to the east. It puzzled me that the female chiru avoided the Aru Basin, and I could only speculate that they followed a traditional migratory route, one used generation after generation. Toward the end of the Pleistocene, when glaciers were lower and lake levels higher, the Aru Basin might have been difficult to traverse. Yet now, ten thousand or more years later, although conditions have changed, the chiru still adhere to their ancient trails, as if they retained an enduring atlas of the Chang Tang.

August 1. The chiru often tarried in a small valley where they rested and fed. In that valley was a knoll and I hid by it. Placing slats of shale on end, I constructed a natural blind and waited motionless, head close to the ground. A breeze blew and the slopes vibrated in the sun. Suddenly a herd of chiru poured into my valley, grunting softly, almost a murmur, a sound I had never before been close enough to hear. A number of females stopped near me, some within about a hundred feet, and began to forage. Their month-old young, tired from the trek, flopped down to rest. A few tried to suckle but their mothers usually turned aside. The females were molting, their woolly coats tattered. While these animals lingered, another chiru wave crested and flowed down upon me. I took a few cautious photographs, and several chiru downwind of me became nervous, but I was a cairn and most animals near me were unconcerned. This reassured the herd and I remained among them for three hours.

At least eight thousand females and young passed down this valley within a few days and more no doubt came after we left for Lhasa. We had been witnesses to one of the last migrations in the Chang Tang. A hundred years ago, tens of thousands of migrating animals had crowded these plains, but they remain ghost herds of memory.

This western migratory population is the largest remaining one in existence, at that time containing, I would guess, at least twenty-five thousand animals, but intensive hunting has surely reduced its numbers since then. Two other migratory herds, both much smaller, persist in the Chang Tang of Tibet and one across the border in Qinghai. These animals, together with various nonmigratory herds, probably now total fewer than seventy-five thousand. They are the last of their species.

October 1993

As we drove to Siling Co and entered the newly established Chang Tang Reserve, I felt a sense of satisfaction. On July 19, 1993, the government of Tibet had passed the final legislation that established the Chang Tang Nature Reserve. It consists officially of 95,095 square miles of reserve with another 14,245 square miles of special protected area adjoining in the west, an area that includes the Aru Basin, for a total of 109,340 square miles. However, careful measurements on maps suggest that the area actually extends over about 128,500 square miles. It is the second largest reserve in the world, exceeded only by one in northern Greenland which consists mostly of ice cap. For comparison, the reserve is about the size of New Mexico or almost as large as Germany. Even so, some chiru still migrate beyond its borders.

To establish this reserve had been a relatively easy administrative matter; to maintain it as a viable ecosystem, unmodified and undegraded, in the decades ahead will be difficult. The administrative permit for the reserve states in part: "Every kind of effective measure must be adopted after the establishment of reserves to protect every species of precious and rare animals that need protection, to make use of the ecological, social, and economic resources with efficiency, to bring the reserves up to national standard."

When we visit a nomad encampment
to discuss livestock and rangeland issues,
everyone crowds around to participate.

The government is obviously concerned about wildlife conservation, but it views the reserve not as wilderness to be set aside as a park but as a multiple-use area where the needs and aspirations of the nomads must be considered.

We all aspire to discover and create and accomplish something beyond ourselves, and I had contributed a significant fragment of my life to this area. My next step would be to help develop management procedures for the reserve, ones that will permit the wild herds, the livestock, and the nomads to coexist in the decades and centuries ahead. I needed to know more about the nomads—their number, amount of livestock, attitudes toward wildlife. Admittedly, I easily contained my enthusiasm for this aspect of the work; I prefer watching animals to interviewing people. But I also realized that the future viability of the reserve depended on the cooperation and participation of the nomads.

There were six of us on this October trip. Ding Li was along, having become my Chang Tang shadow as companion and interpreter. I had also brought Daniel Miller, a range ecologist who speaks Tibetan, learned during years in Nepal, to evaluate the condition of the steppe and assess livestock management practices. With his Stetson, bandanna, boots, and mustache, a reminder of his ranching past in Montana, he fitted well into these rangelands. I enjoyed the rare pleasure of having a colleague with whom to share ideas and discuss data. October is perhaps the cruelest

month in the Chang Tang: the weather looks tranquil and seductive, with the sky cloudless and temperatures seldom below zero, but the wind rages so relentlessly out of the west each day that after an outing we gratefully retreated to car or village room, heads throbbing and bodies stiff from the assault.

It had been my impression that the rangelands in the Chang Tang Reserve as a whole remained in excellent condition, and Dan Miller agreed. The challenge now was to keep them that way.

Many nomads told us about their lives and their concerns regarding livestock and wildlife. The leader of Rongma, So Da, briefed us about his administrative unit, or *xiang*. It has 83 families with 488 people and they own 1059 yaks—used mainly as beasts of burden—174 horses, and 39,121 sheep and goats, or about 486 animals per household. The sheep supply wool and meat, and the goats produce milk and cashmere. The value of cashmere has recently increased rapidly on the international market, bringing ten times the price of wool, and as a result many families are increasing the proportion of goats in their flocks. Each person is allowed seventy sheep or goats or a combination of other livestock on the basis of one yak equals five sheep. However, rules are somewhat lax here because grass is ample. Farther south, where grass is in short supply, the livestock limit is only forty head per person; excess animals must be sold to the government. The *xiang* buys most of the wool from the families at prices somewhat lower than those offered by private traders, but few such traders come this far north. The government in turn sells barley for making *tsamba* at subsidized low prices. Some families are wealthy, with up to two thousand sheep, whereas a few are so poor that they require government assistance. Conditions are good at Rongma now, So Da concluded, and he does not want more people.

This recitation of facts reveals a nomad society that is closely regulated by the government and a local economy that is controlled by national and international forces. Most families live reasonably well, as measured by local standards, and some have enough income to hire others to help with construction of corrals and slaughter of sheep in late autumn. The endless array of subsistence tasks remains part of the daily routine, of herding livestock regardless of weather, in rain, hail, and cold, alone, all day every day, of milking and collecting yak chips. But in some ways the nomads' lives have eased. Trucks bring supplies to the *xiang* and purchase livestock products, making month-long trips by yak caravan unnecessary. A cash economy enables people to buy everything from watches, bicycles, and radios to sewing machines and even houses.

When, that October, we again visited Pujung Narla near the hot springs, his tents were still there, but there was also a new three-room house with a roof of poplar poles and bamboo covered with a layer of earth. The government had hauled in the building materials without cost but Pujung Narla had to pay for them. Other nomads, too, had built themselves houses in the five years since I began work in this area. The houses served as storage sheds, places to lock up possessions, and retreats during the bitter winter. Tibetan tents are flimsy and drafty, poorly adapted to winter and far inferior to the cozy, well-designed, and mobile Mongolian gers, or yurts. My mind accepted Pujung Narla's house as wholly sensible, whereas my heart could not rid itself of the image of the freedom of a nomad's life in a tent. Houses imply permanence, no matter how strong the commitment to traditional values and customs, and I wondered what long-term impact they would have. Would nomads now graze livestock nearer home to the detriment of the range? Would they try to "improve" pastures by bringing in exotic grasses? Would they fence everything?

Whatever the future, we were grateful to Pujung Narla for offering us shelter in his house. But we depended on ourselves for food. With us was Lu Wei as representative from the Tibet Forest Bureau; from Sichuan, he had an insatiable appetite for pigs, specifically pig heads. Since he had purchased all the trip's supplies, we had boxes of flattened pig heads that looked as if processed by a ten-ton truck. The best that could be said for them was that sliced pig ear is chewy. When boiled, most heads had an aged aroma: we sniffed and declined. "Why don't you like pig heads?" asked Lu Wei plaintively as he ate. "In Sichuan they are a delicacy." When he threw the remains of a head out the door, two lean dogs rushed up. One at a time they too sniffed and declined.

As we approached Garco, we saw another sign of change: a fence. Most *xiangs* have in recent years fenced a pasture or two to save fodder for the winter, especially for horses, but Bema, Garco's party secretary, who had a fondness for status-enhancing projects, was building a huge barrier that stretched for miles to enclose an entire valley. Was this fence emblematic of the Chang Tang's future? Open rangelands, where wildlife could wander hundreds of miles without obstruction, could vanish, as they did on the American prairies. Fences will doom the roving wild herds; only some gazelles might survive. Progress in the government's policy of increasing livestock production was now measured in miles of fence, I was told. A *xiang* had to pay only 20 percent of the fence's cost.

On reaching Garco, I noted that the village had built a *chorten,* or stupa, a small temple, symbolic of the earth's five elements —earth, water, fire, air, and ether—and a reminder of the Buddhist cycle of birth and rebirth. This white *chorten* added a new aura to the village and it provided an interesting juxtaposition to the derelict white dish antenna. We asked Dawa, Garco's official leader, what he thought of the new reserve. "The government established the reserve. I have no opinion," he said, obviously deferring to the party secretary in everything. Bema noted that "there is lots of space for wildlife up north." I pointed out that space up north is indeed ample, but grass is not and that many wild animals depend on his *xiang* for survival. "Most wildlife is no problem," Bema continued, except for wild yak bulls which sometimes injure people, drive off domestic yak cows, and break down fences. He has had to shoot two of them. He felt that it was too much responsibility for him to protect wildlife unless the government paid for it. Shuanghu had been provided with some funds for distribution to the *xiangs* by the Tibet Forest Bureau and Beijing's Ministry of Forestry for just that purpose, we told Bema. He was not pleased with our pointed queries and comments.

We asked many nomads questions about their attitude toward wildlife. "It is good to protect wildlife. But we would like to hunt the *zhi* [chiru] because we are poor," said one. "Why are there limits on my livestock when there are several hundred kiang in the area? Kiang are useless but eat much grass," said another. But a third nomad said simply, "I like to see wild animals around." Whatever the sentiment now, most nomads, like ranchers anywhere in the world, could become less tolerant of wildlife if competition for forage with livestock is perceived as being serious.

ABOVE: The Garco commune consists of two villages, this one located in a valley of the Aru Range. A *chorten*—"a receptacle for offerings" in Tibetan—stands at the edge of the village where nomads circle it in a clockwise direction as a daily religious observance.

RIGHT: Range ecologist Daniel Miller interviews a nomad about the condition of the grasslands.

The kiang is already in such disfavor that some *xiangs* have petitioned the government for permission to shoot them. "I would be happy if there were no kiangs," a nomad told me. I reminded him that average kiang density is low, that the large herds are only temporary aggregations during winter. Though I may like to see a kiang herd gallop along with the car and suddenly wheel like a well-trained cavalry squadron to line up and watch us with curiosity, only to bolt and repeat the maneuver, my enjoyment does not solve the problem of many kiang grazing on winter pasture that a family has saved for its sheep and goats.

During my months in the Chang Tang, I made a special effort to study the food habits of wildlife and livestock to learn how much the diet of the various species overlap. Since there are few varieties of plants, and coverage is sparse, the herbivores have a limited choice, most of it grass and sedge. The wild herbivores have obviously avoided serious competition or they would not have persisted together for millennia, but the four domestic species are a recent intrusion. The wild species have to some extent divided the landscape among themselves with blue sheep, argalis, and yaks mainly in the hills, and chiru, kiang, and gazelle on the plains, although each may move to any habitat in search of high-quality forage. The domestic species also feed in all types of terrain.

The six wild herbivores overlap greatly in the plant species they eat but they differ in the proportion of plant types, whether grass, herb, or shrub. Large animals such as yaks and kiang need large amounts of food and they are, therefore, mainly grazers. Kiang in particular consume much bulk, including coarse grass stems, because like all equids they digest food poorly. Medium-sized animals, such as chiru, argali, and blue sheep, obtain a nutritional balance by selecting a variety of foods, the amount of each depending on the season. Because of its small size the Tibetan gazelle has a higher metabolism than the other species, and it therefore needs the most nutritious forage. Since grasses are generally of lower food quality than herbs, gazelles mainly select the latter, picking only the best morsels.

Is there competition? With wildlife populations now well below what they once were, competition for forage is not evident, even in winter when high-quality forage is scarce. In fact, competition may have been what shaped this community of animals so different in body size and with different terrain preferences. I can only observe the end product of a long evolutionary history, a community from which selection may have excluded others long ago.

Domestic yaks and horses are, as can be expected, mostly grazers. Sheep and goats also eat much grass but they consume other plant types as well. In general, wild and domestic species of a certain size eat the same plants in roughly similar proportions, and this creates a potentially competitive

Lone herders are usually pleased to interrupt the tedium of watching their sheep and goats to answer our questions about wildlife and livestock. This herdsman had a kitten for a companion.

situation. However, livestock numbers in the reserve have not yet increased to a level where food shortages exist. Even heavy grazing has not caused range deterioration, because most of it occurs in winter when grasses and sedges are senescent, having stored their nutrients underground.

Still, the nomads' complaints about kiang are based on fact: the kiang do in a few localities have an impact on the amount of grass available to livestock. The critical words here are "in a few localities." Management issues must be resolved at a local level, in specific places, not by sweeping policies that affect the reserve as a whole.

Our survey that October showed that about four thousand nomad families, comprising twenty-two thousand people, depend on the reserve either seasonally or throughout the year. These families have an estimated 1.4 million head of livestock of which 64 percent are sheep, 29 percent goats, 6 percent yaks, and 1 percent horses, or a density of eleven animals per square mile. Compared to all that livestock, average density of wild hoofed animals was actually very low, roughly 103,000 animals or 0.8 per square mile. But such a comparison for the whole reserve is of limited use because half has little or no livestock. Both wildlife and livestock concentrate on the fine steppe of feather grass, especially in the eastern part. Within this area of about 35,250 square miles, there were about 1.0 wild and 22.7 domestic hoofed animals per

square mile, the wild animals comprising only 4.2 percent of the total. Of course, a gazelle or sheep is not the equivalent of a yak in size or amount of forage it eats. If I compute the biomass, or total weight, of each species, then wildlife represents just 10.4 percent. By either measure, livestock greatly exceeds the amount of wildlife. (The number of domestic animals—1.4 million—also gives an indication of the huge herds of chiru and kiang and wild yaks that the region could and probably once did support.)

The human population is certain to grow considerably as the many children in the nomad families mature and create their own households. Since most nomad children remain illiterate, the future offers them mainly a pastoral life. With more people, domestic animals, houses, roads, and fences the Chang Tang will be much modified, and the wildlife that remains will find it increasingly difficult to adapt.

Nomads,
Past and Present

The Tibetan nomads, or *drokba*, were, and to some extent still are, viewed by some Westerners as living an exotic and legendary life unchanged for centuries. Freedom to roam these uplands with their livestock for over a millennium has supposedly imbued them with the wisdom of ages, their simple lifestyle serving as a beacon away from our complicated lives. I presume that such romantic visions cause no harm if they lead to an appreciation of a resilient and hardy people. But the Tibetans in the reserve are not part of a pastoral theme park and their lives are not static, fixed in time—nor have they ever been.

Tibetan nomads were not free to seek their own destiny in the past. For centuries the powerful aristocratic families and incarnate lamas of various monasteries controlled the people, even in the Chang Tang two hundred or more miles from any population center. Nomads had to pay taxes to their overlord in the form of butter and had to sell wool to him at depressed prices. They were not free to leave his estates and were bound by heredity to remain. Each family was allocated certain pastures, their size depending on the amount of livestock and carrying capacity of each range. A family had exclusive rights to these pastures for three years, after which they were

reallocated on the basis of an increase or decrease in livestock numbers. The Chang Tang, far from being a land of free-roaming nomads, was divided into a mosaic of precisely delineated grazing plots occupied, in effect, by small-time ranchers.

After Tibet's old society came to an end in 1959 with the flight of the Dalai Lama to India and the assumption of complete power by China, the lives of the nomads continued with only minor disruptions until the late 1960s and the arrival of the Cultural Revolution. Wealthy nomads became "class enemies," private ownership of livestock was abolished, religious practices were barred, and all nomads were forced into communes. Melvyn Goldstein and Cynthia Beall write: "Chinese policy during this period sought to maintain pastoral production but destroy the social and cultural fabric of the nomads' traditional way of life. From the nomads' point of view, they had become an exploited subject class treated far worse than they had been under the 'serfdom' of the old society." Conditions improved after Mao Zedong's death in 1976, and reforms led to the abolition of communes in 1981 and their replacement by local administrative centers, the *xiangs*.

When communes were disbanded, every person—man, woman, and child—received

An infant has been swaddled and stuffed into a cradle made of kiang hide, leaving the child motionless except for its eyes. Tibet has the highest reproductive rate in China, with an average of 4.3 children per couple. Almost every encampment has a lively swarm of children.

Within the same encampment are traditional nomads and others who have adopted modern clothes, wear watches, and ride bicycles. Both retain basically the old style of life. At left, a nomad calculates his expected payment from the sale of sheep wool to a trader.

the same share of livestock. As in any society, some prospered and others failed and within ten years there were again rich and poor nomads. Garco remained an exception in that its people voted to remain a commune, the only one in Tibet.

During most of these years the area that is now the Chang Tang Reserve remained almost uninhabited. The few explorers who had crossed from the north a hundred years before usually met no one until they reached the vicinity of Shuanghu and Garco or even Siling Co. But one of the world's last great grasslands could not long remain hidden and untouched. During the mid-1970s the government prodded communities to move north and establish themselves at Rongma, Tsasang, and Garco, and it built Shuanghu into an administrative center. For the first time sharp-edged buildings disrupted the flow of the terrain, and roads—usually no more than two parallel ruts—penetrated valleys where once only wild yaks had trod. Development had begun.

The general attitude of Tibetan and Chinese officials toward traditional grazing practices was dismissive, based on the notion that nomads are inefficient and backward. Livestock production could be increased, the officials felt, only by using scientific methods, but just what these might entail is still unclear because no long-term research has been conducted.

The useful practice of periodic pasture reallocation was discarded in 1959. This traditional system did not serve all pasture-lands equally well, judging by long-standing degradation and erosion evident in, for example, parts of southern Tibet and eastern Qinghai where communities are large and livestock numbers great. But it did seem to have functioned well on the sparsely settled steppe of the Chang Tang.

The new system tries to prevent over-grazing by placing limits on the amount of livestock each person may own. In the past, nomads tried to increase their herds as insurance against calamities, such as the heavy snowstorm of 1985 in Qinghai when many animals died, and as a surplus to eat and trade. Now many lack this buffer of extra animals. Since lambs are born in February and kids in March when winter is still severe, even normal mortality of newborns is high, as high as 40 percent. If the Tibetan *xiang* leader feels that ranges are overstocked, he may arbitrarily order a reduction of herds. The perception among some nomads is that the new system is the government's way of keeping them poor. I also suspect that the current policy may harm wildlife in certain situations because a family with a limit on livestock is more likely to hunt gazelle and chiru to supplement its meat supply. A combination of the old and new systems could perhaps lead to viable range management.

The life of a nomad family revolves around sheep and goats, which must be herded all day every day and brought close to the tent at night for protection. Women do most camp work such as milking, making cheese and butter, and collecting dung for fuel. Yaks and horses are allowed to roam freely over the range, but men herd female yaks to camp daily for milking.

ABOVE: A boy joyfully rides a yak calf. At right, a girl is dressed in her finery, including a decorated dagger and tinderbox. Her necklace is of coral, agate, and turquoise, the last a symbol of good luck.

RIGHT: A toddler stands by a container used to carry water from a stream. The snow is red with the blood of slaughtered sheep.

My strange foreign presence has made the girl above uneasy. At left, a boy wears a cap made from the fur of red fox, one of many subsistence uses of wildlife.

When nomads shift camp, they traditionally
travel by horse. Yaks carry the heavy and
bulky loads such as tents, tent poles, sacks
of barley, and household goods. Today the
administrative units and even some herders
own trucks, and these are often used to
move to new, distant grazing grounds.

On this highland humans and nature
      coexist harmoniously!
The land where spiritual and human law
      reign supreme,
In the land where celestial powers are revered,
Where animals are partners in life's struggle,
Where birds fly without fear,
Where fish swim in freedom,
Where wildlife is protected,
Where men and women cherish inner peace
      and outer freedom.

Tibetan folk song
Quoted by Lobsang Lhalungpa,
Tibet, The Sacred Realm, 1983

After collecting salt at a saline lake in
Tibet, this yak caravan crossed the
border into the Dolpo region of Nepal
to barter for barley and other food in
the lowlands. I photographed this scene
in 1973. Since then the salt caravans in
the Chang Tang and other parts of
Tibet have almost ceased to exist, trade
by truck being more economical.

June 1994

In 1991 I had been a month too late
to find the chiru calving grounds in
the central Chang Tang, and I had
also failed in the west in 1992. It
therefore seemed only reasonable
to try once more, this time with a
third migratory population, one
that wintered around Garco and
Tsasang. It was late May 1994, and
once more we headed north of
Shuanghu. The Tibetans on this
trip called me Gepo, the Old One,
although I was only in my early
sixties, perhaps because it seemed
that I had been following chiru
forever. There were ten of us,

including Kay, Ding Li, Daniel Miller, and driver Danzhen, all of whom had been with me previously. Representing the Tibet Forest Bureau was Liu Wulin, whose cheerful enthusiasm for the work was refreshing. Two Tibetans from the forest police, who planned to check on illegal activities in the region, were also with us.

The journey started well in that we found several herds of pregnant chiru heading north, the tail-end of the migration. Then our truck driver, Tashi Tseren, bogged down, exhibiting what proved to be an unerring homing ability for any soft ground, no matter how scarce. Dan and I skipped the excavation and walked ahead.

About fifty chiru dashed, tightly bunched, up an embankment, and racing behind them was a shaggy wolf. It barely kept pace as the females swept together in a large arc around us onto a low ridge. When the herd dipped briefly out of sight, the wolf closed the gap in a blur of speed with a shortcut. One chiru veered aside and stood like a spectator at a race, and the wolf passed her by. Then another female left the safety of the herd in a panic; the wolf focused on her, pulling her down in a cloud of dust, and, as later examination showed, bit her through the top of the skull.

After camping for the night at Linggo Co, we ascended toward a seventeen-thousand-foot pass close to Purog Kangri, the pale ice cap of this massif barely discernible in the luminous haze. Over four hundred chiru females were at the pass, heading northeast.

Just beyond this pass, Dan spotted a man far up on the slope of the mountain. We wondered what he was doing so far from any pastoral areas. On reaching the spot near where we had seen him, we found a freshly skinned chiru. Above us, in a dip of the hills, were ten domestic yaks and two horses, and two men were hurriedly dismantling a tent as if to hide; a third man joined them. Their camp looked like the lair of a berserk butcher, strewn with chiru carcasses, disconnected heads, slabs of meat, three chiru fetuses, and hides stretched out to dry. Most prominent was the head of a wild yak bull, the animal having been killed, we were told, with a fusillade of forty shots. (The men had bought two small-bore rifles from the Bureau of Animal Husbandry for protection against wolves.) The three men were brothers from a village near Shuanghu. Like everyone else we met, they were familiar with the wildlife laws, but one brother, who had been a trader, had gone bankrupt, owed money, and hoped to recoup his losses by killing chiru. So far they had shot nine chiru and the yak. They planned to take the hides to Shuanghu and sell them for the equivalent of at least thirty dollars each to one of the traders who go there to buy sheep and goat wool. Our two policemen made an inventory, confiscated the rifles, and ordered the brothers to report to the Shuanghu authorities. Later I learned that they had been fined $1765, to be paid in sheep wool and other products.

PRECEDING PAGES: In the eastern part of the reserve, the Purog Kangri massif rises on the horizon to nearly twenty-three thousand feet. I am looking for a ford that will permit our vehicles to cross.

The steppe polecat subsists mainly on pikas. It is a close relative and the ecological equivalent of America's critically endangered black-footed ferret, which depends on prairie dogs. Pikas and prairie dogs have both been blamed for eating grass that ranchers want for their livestock, and they have both been subjected to poisoning campaigns. A polecat population needs large pika colonies to maintain itself, and such colonies exist mainly on the lush meadowlands east of the Chang Tang. I never saw a polecat in the reserve.

We settled for a few days along the Zhang Shui He, Long Water River, which flows north into Dogai Coring, a lake I had visited briefly in 1991. It is a long lake, forty-five miles east to west, and we reasoned that the chiru surely had to migrate via one side or the other. So we checked the eastern side almost to the Qinghai border, finding all routes difficult because of several glacier-fed rivers. Nothing. We moved camp and checked the western side, traveling northward past Rola Kangri, a glacier peak, to another lake, Dogaicoring Qangco, and further to the north where from a forbiddingly barren range we could scan the Koko Xili, a series of peaks not far from the Xinjiang border. Of the females there was no sign; it seemed somehow preordained that they would foil us yet again.

I could only speculate that the chiru had migrated east along the slopes of Purog Kangri into Qinghai and then moved north, taking a path we lacked the gasoline to follow. Just as in the Aru Basin, their route had no topographic logic if viewed through today's eyes. Instead the chiru seemed to retain an inner logic from a time when Dogai Coring was much larger and the most suitable high ground for travel was to the east. Siling Co, for example, is at present 520 square miles in size, but judging by old beach lines it was once almost five times as big

That June was dry, except for occasional snow and hail, and the steppe remained desiccated, the grass still yellow and winter-brittle.

Winds raked the plains, one gust carrying away a camp tent which team members chased for three futile miles. Wildlife avoided the area; in fact the plains were so empty that something seemed amiss. Then I realized that the pikas were almost gone. Pika holes were abundant, but they had the uncared-for appearance of an abandoned home. We were in a vast city of the dead, hundreds or even thousands of square miles in size, a Pompeii where some catastrophe had terminated the flow of life. A mass exodus is unlikely. In other parts of the plateau, pikas are being poisoned with zinc phosphide because they are thought to compete with livestock for forage, but surely not here. A plague must have swept through the colonies, and deprived of food, predatory birds and mammals were now scarce as well.

Just to the north of these plains, the Rola Kangri terminates at its eastern end in high, rounded hills. In striking contrast to the plains, their slopes were green with grass growing among the volcanic rocks. Blue and yellow irises flowered in protected nooks, and various herbs had emerged. All this fresh forage had attracted many male chiru as well as a few kiang. In drainages wild yaks gathered to graze on the sedge meadows, and we tallied 437, more than in any area except the Aru Basin. Green forage may contain up to 20 percent protein, whereas during the long winter months protein levels are at or below the 6 percent that animals need to maintain

The white-lipped deer is confined to the
Tibetan Plateau where it prefers alpine
uplands. The species reaches only the
easternmost edge of the Chang Tang but
does not extend into the reserve. It is
heavily hunted for its antlers, which are
used in traditional medicines, yet herds
with a hundred or more animals can still
be seen in a few areas of eastern Qinghai.

Flowers are relatively sparse and inconspicuous on the steppe that covers most of
the reserve. But along the southeastern
edge, where moist meadows are extensive,
flowers often add brilliant colors to the
alpine gardens. There are several species of
gentian (right), an intensely bright louse-
wort (above), and a spiny-leafed blue poppy
(top) which tends to grow in places where
the soil has been disturbed by livestock or
erosion. A short-stemmed iris (top right)
is one of the first spring flowers in June.

themselves. These hills, green two to three weeks before other areas, were extremely important to wildlife as a place to replenish their energy, rear young, mate, and fulfill other imperatives. We established a small satellite camp at the base of these hills to study vegetation and wildlife, but I primarily remember the area for its bears.

Here pikas had survived in abundance, and perhaps the bears had congregated to feed on them. It was also the bears' mating season, another good reason for a get-together. We met at least eleven different bears, a number that may seem small, but attests to the rarity of the animals elsewhere.

June 15. Two bears were on a gentle slope. One was large, probably a male, with fur the color of straw on his neck and sides; the other, presumably a female, was small and dark. The male rested, chin on forepaws. The female was 150 feet from him, digging for pikas by sweeping the silt and sand sideways and back, her head so deep in the hole that only her hindquarters were visible. Ten feet from her, watching intently, and ready to pounce on any pika that might escape her, was a white wolf. Having caught nothing, the bear meandered past five burrows, pausing briefly at each to sniff if anyone was home, and the wolf tagged along. At the next hole she dug again. The male ambled up and reclined beside her. Busily shoveling soil, she ignored him. The fact that she even tolerated him indicated that they were a courting couple.

The wolf stood next to them. I was uncertain if she caught anything because she would gulp a pika whole. The female walked —the wolf her white shadow—and trailing behind was the male. Then both bears dug while the wolf waited by each in turn. The wolf's patience was not rewarded during the hour I watched. However, wolves must occasionally obtain a free pika snack, because I saw the two carnivores associate like this three other times.

Babu wanted to go home. He was a policeman from Nagqu and also the driver of one of our cars, both jobs of such status in China that his demand was seriously heeded. Divisive and arrogant, he coveted one of the confiscated rifles and tried to bribe the others to let him have it. His refrain *"buxing"* (roughly meaning "not possible") was so constant that we used it as an epithet when referring to him among ourselves. But we had sufficient supplies and gasoline for one more long survey trip and insisted on doing it. Traveling northwest of Dogai Coring, we crossed hills that were utterly desolate; in the first thirty miles I spotted only one animal, a chiru male. Late in the day we reached the Yako Basin, also known as Pamachungtsong. In a hundred miles of driving we had found only one site with fresh water, a small seepage, and the Yako Basin was dry, its lake an alkali flat. But luckily we discovered a small stream at the basin's southern margin, a stream that had its source in three springs.

By the springs were old stone tools and recent stone corrals, indicating that the site had a long history of human use. Nomads need adequate grazing and fresh water—sheep and goats must drink at least once every two days—and the Yako Basin was an oasis of both. The government had moved several families into the area in 1978, but they remained only a year before returning south, the isolation and scarcity of water too much for them. Once again the area belonged to the wild animals.

Along one edge of the Yako Basin are a number of rounded rock outcrops, or kopjes, and among them we found a herd of nine Tibetan argali rams, their horns large and curled. Argalis are one of the rarest sights in the Chang Tang. They are partial to high rolling hills, a widespread habitat on the plateau, yet the animals are rare and local, a few here and there with vast seemingly suitable tracts devoid of them. Their mysterious scarcity could not be blamed on meat hunters; I seldom encountered even an argali's skull.

But I certainly had no difficulty in finding yak skulls. In the Yako Basin, I counted fifty-five skulls, most without other bones, indicating that the animals had been butchered. Perhaps some of the skulls remained from the days of the ill-conceived settlement, but most others were probably from the official Shuanghu hunting expeditions which continued at least until 1990. The species has long had full protection in China and by interna-tional convention, and I was filled with indig-nation that it was still so casually persecuted even deep in its last stronghold.

Animals are not just simple images but a tangle of cultural ideas, a mix of illusion and fact. To Nikolai Przewalski in the 1870s, the yaks, so big, bold, and impressive, were some-thing to subdue: "We left the greater number of those we shot untouched, having no use for meat in Tibet." But he also rhapsodized about them: "In these inhospitable wastes, in the midst of a desolate nature, yet far removed from pitiless man, the famous long-haired ox roams in unrestricted freedom." Over a century later, in 1991, Ma Lihua wrote in her book *Glimpses of Northern Tibet* how "on a trip in the west we ran across a few wild yaks; we shot at them for all we were worth." She conveyed nothing about the animals other than that they were targets.

I carry with me several images of the yak, on one level as meat, tents, and other local commodities, and on another level as an icon, a totem of this harsh and lonely land. I real-ize that my mind has appropriated and trans-formed the animal, creating a myth. But a myth can become a new reality, and the yak is a creature to treasure. Being a naturalist with empathy for animals is in some ways a curse: it creates concern and guilt and robs one of simple enjoyment. Whenever I met yaks I was haunted by the thought of their extinction, of their fleeting time on our shared earth, unless attitudes toward them soon change.

For unknown reasons, Tibetan argali sheep are rare in the reserve, and we seldom found their massive skulls. Horn rings show that this ram was about seven and a half years old when he died.

The wild yak does indeed need "unrestricted freedom," as Przewalski stated, large tracts in which nomads are sparse or absent. Domestic and wild yaks readily hybridize, and the pure wild strain will vanish with frequent contact, assuming any survive the meat hunters and livestock diseases.

At one time yaks occurred throughout the treeless highlands of the plateau, but in the past hundred years their range has steadily contracted as nomads took the best pastures for their livestock. Except for a few small and scattered populations with scant future, yaks now survive mainly in the Chang Tang, particularly in the Chang Tang Reserve.

I attempted to estimate wild yak numbers in the reserve. Only two areas, around the Aru Basin and Dogai Coring, had relatively many, whereas in most others there were few to very few. A rough estimate for the reserve was up to eight thousand. Yaks also survive in other parts of the Chang Tang, as well as in the Arjin Shan Reserve, the Qilian Shan of northeast Qinghai, and a few other spots. Perhaps fifteen thousand persist on the entire Tibetan Plateau. During the Ice Age, wild yaks had a wide distribution in central Asia, as far north as eastern Russia. No one knows when or where they were domesticated. But it is ironic that the last wild yaks, so impressively large and so filled with vital tension, now cling to their final refuge, while their domestic descendants, small and phlegmatic by comparison, rule by the millions.

A yak herd has concentrated on a moist patch of alpine meadow where it has cropped the sedges and herbs to within half an inch of the ground (opposite). Yaks favor such sites because forage there is nutritious. Bulls, such as the four above, often form small bachelor herds. After the Aru region, the area around Dogai Coring in the east has the largest yak population in the reserve.

Epilogue

Our journeys through the Chang Tang revealed three ecological zones. The southern third of the reserve, with its good pastures, has been settled by nomads mostly during the past thirty to forty years. In that brief span, the wild yaks have been almost exterminated, but this steppe remains important as the favored habitat of kiang and Tibetan gazelles, and the northern edge is critical for chiru in winter. North of that is a broad zone that has adequate pastures in only a few places and these the nomads use either seasonally or have

occasionally tried to settle. But scarcity of fresh water and pasture has deterred human intrusion. Here most yaks and a modest number of other animals survive. Along the northern edge of the reserve is a desert with such meager resources that nomads and most wildlife avoid it. Only chiru females make seasonal forays there.

In just a few years I witnessed the relentless attrition of wildlife. I observed the past die, and looking ahead could see only an empty steppe. I also knew that there was still time to develop a plan that would permit harmony between wildlife, livestock, and people. But immediate action is required, before the wildlife is further decimated and other serious conservation problems arise. After our 1993 and 1994 trips, Dan Miller and I made several suggestions to the government that are now being considered, among them:

- The current level of illegal commercial hunting is wholly unsustainable. Wildlife laws must be strictly enforced or the reserve will lose that for which it was explicitly established. Patrol efforts should be increased with emphasis on apprehending traders and other middlemen.
- The uninhabited central and northern areas are at best marginal for livestock production. They should be wholly reserved for wildlife and even brief human access prohibited except by permit.
- Building long fences that impede the free

movement of wildlife should be banned.
- Some areas need to be closed, at least during certain seasons. For example, chiru court at traditional sites but human disturbance disrupts them and livestock depletes available forage there. The Aru Basin provides the finest wildlife spectacle in the Chang Tang, yet a few nomad families are in the process of destroying this national treasure. Use of the basin by nomads should be carefully regulated.
- Population growth will make sustainable management of resources in the reserve increasingly difficult. To limit such growth, further immigration should be prohibited.
- Instituting a conservation education program is essential to convey the spiritual and economic benefits of good resource management. Such a program should involve monks, biologists, economists, range managers, anthropologists, and others.

A conservation problem is seldom clear-cut, a solution invariably complex as principles and practicalities are juggled. Conservation is like Hydra, the many-headed serpent of myth that grew two heads whenever one was cut off. New problems are constantly added to the old. When I first visited Shuanghu in 1988, fences were not an issue. In 1993, as I spoke with Vice Governor Tsering Wangay, he casually said, "There is expected to be oil in the Shuanghu area." Oil drilling would require detailed regulations to prevent spills,

PRECEDING PAGES: A herdsman guides his flock along a grassy shoreline where waves of a lake lapped several millennia ago.

154

Hunters once came from Shuanghu
to shoot wild yaks by the truckload,
leaving the heads behind. A yak's
black hair fades to brown after years
of exposure to the elements.

The wild and bleak Chang Tang, austere yet tranquil, seemingly empty but not lonely.

unnecessary roads, discarded equipment, and other environmental damage, as has occurred so excessively at Prudhoe Bay in northern Alaska in recent years. And an influx of outsiders could lead to much illegal hunting. The following year, I saw several new oil-drilling rigs just east of Siling Co outside the reserve, and two oil exploration teams were in the reserve that summer.

In 1994, on the road from Baingoin to Nyima, we met a caravan of about fifty small tractors, each loaded with bundles, shovels, cans of extra fuel, and four to five Chinese, most of them Hui, a Muslim group. They were going to Nyima, where there had been a gold strike along the reserve's southern border. Two to three thousand diggers had already passed through. During the past few years, gold seekers had also invaded the Arjin Shan Reserve and penetrated the Chang Tang of Qinghai, where they decimated the wildlife.

The Chang Tang attracted me because of its unique wildlife. But I soon became immersed in the complex problems of biodiversity conservation, environmental protection, economic development, and welfare of a traditional culture. My research results were fragmentary, and, as in any project, they raised more issues and asked more questions than they could hope to answer. There is still little known about the way in which the wild and domestic herbivores, from pikas to yaks, use and affect the steppe. Accurate wildlife censuses need to be conducted and the populations then monitored year to year.

Surveys of livestock should be made intermittently to detect, for example, changes in land use and herding practices and to assess the economics of marketing livestock products.

But one fact remains an insistent presence: unregulated hunting has decimated one of the world's great wildlife populations. To halt the decline and reverse the trend would require the long-term interest, skills, and involvement of the nomads. Without a positive attitude toward wildlife and an incentive to protect it and the rangelands, the nomads would increasingly view wild animals as competitors and continue to regard them as a source of food and income. The challenge is to devise a means of benefiting people from the presence of wildlife, a challenge unfortunately so difficult that success stories are still all too rare. Tourism is sometimes viewed as a panacea for natural areas. If properly managed, tourism can assist a local economy and stimulate conservation. But the Chang Tang Reserve is too remote and too high to entice many tourists. What other options are there?

Perhaps after wildlife has been allowed to increase, subsistence hunting for kiang, blue sheep, and others could be allowed, a strictly regulated harvest that would benefit all nomads, not just a small percentage as the illegal kill does now. It is, however, the chiru that has the greatest economic potential because of the luxury market for its wool. How ironic that I worked for years to help chiru and now conclude that in the future

they might be sustainably culled commercially for wool, meat, and horns! A combination of chiru and livestock management could also lead to good management of rangelands with nomads careful to maintain the chiru's habitat. After all, a chiru is more valuable than a sheep. The primary objective in managing the reserve as a multi-use area is to maintain an undamaged ecosystem with viable populations of all native plants and animals, as well as to offer the nomads the economic benefits that will permit them to continue their traditional lives. The chiru might just make this possible.

The Chinese refer to Tibet as Xizang, the Western Treasure House. They probably think in terms of gold, yet the real treasure is the land, with its golden vistas and peaks in perpetual winter, its cushions of flowers, vibrant chiru and yak herds, and wild winds. The establishment of the Chang Tang Reserve was a remarkable conservation initiative by the Tibet Autonomous Region and China. At the end of this century, one that has seen greater environmental destruction than any other in history, few countries still have large, relatively undamaged ecosystems. The Chang Tang is one of these, and now that it has been given a measure of protection, humans, livestock, and wildlife can live there in the ecological harmony that is the basis of Tibetan Buddhism.

We all, not just nomads and the Tibet government, are responsible for the fate of the reserve. The nomads produce wool to subsist, and it is of such high quality that carpet and other industries prize it. The fate also rests with traders, manufacturers, and shop owners who deal in the wool. And finally it depends on those wealthy enough to buy carpets and other products, who affect the lives of people and animals so remote that they may never have heard of them. As His Holiness the Dalai Lama wrote in 1990:

> Central to Buddha's teaching is seeing the equality among human beings and the importance of equality of all sentient beings. Whether you are a Buddhist or not, this is something important to know and to understand. . . .
>
> Nature and wild animals are complementary. People who live among wildlife without harming it are in harmony with the environment. Some of that harmony remains in Tibet, and because we had this in the past, we have some genuine hope for the future. If we make an attempt, we can have all this again.

Tibetans have from time immemorial maintained wildlife sanctuaries around temples and in special preserves of the mountain gods. The Chang Tang Reserve is a natural temple on a grand scale, a monument to Tibet's past, a sanctuary where the faithful can find inspiration. According to a Tibetan proverb the experience of emptiness engenders compassion. What better place to achieve both than in the Chang Tang? The nomads would betray their own wisdom if they failed to maintain the reserve as an eternal gift to the future.

For about nine hundred years the Tibetans have revered Milarepa, a hermit, philosopher, and poet who had supreme contempt for worldly possessions. As he lay dying, he exhorted his disciples:

> Do if you like that which may seem sinful
> But help living beings,
> Because that is truly pious work.

ABOVE: Will the region's nomads retain their commitment to traditional values and customs?

LEFT: In the lingering light of a subzero day, a female Tibetan gazelle reclines in the white immensity of the eastern Chang Tang.

OVERLEAF: Two nomads ride across the vastness of a plain empty of wildlife. Will that be the future of the whole Chang Tang? The reserve needs to receive international recognition as a World Heritage Site and Biosphere Reserve.

Selected Reading

The fascinating history of Tibet and Tibetans during the past 1500 years is best described in these two books, both by authors who knew Tibet intimately:

Bell, Sir Charles. 1924 (reprinted 1968). *Tibet past and present*. Oxford University Press, London.

Richardson, Hugh. 1984. *Tibet and its history*. Shambhala, Boulder.

The history of Tibet during the first half of this century is complex and not always accurately presented. This thorough book gives the facts:

Goldstein, Melvyn. 1989. *A history of modern Tibet, 1913–1951*. University of California Press, Berkeley.

Tibet has changed dramatically in recent decades. The following two books have many old photographs that offer poignant glimpses of the past, people, monasteries, and other aspects of an old culture:

Lhalungpa, Lobsang. 1983. *Tibet, the sacred realm*. Aperture Press, New York.

Normanton, Simon. 1989. *Tibet, the lost civilisation*. Penguin Books, London.

Several explorers crossed the Chang Tang, traveling through or near the area that is now the Chang Tang Reserve. Their accounts, all ninety or more years old, well describe the landscapes, wildlife, and hardships of this high and harsh land. I often retraced part of the routes of these explorers and could directly compare their observations with mine:

Bower, Hamilton. 1894 (reprinted 1976). *Diary of a journey across Tibet*. Ratna Pustak Bhandar Publ., Kathmandu, Nepal.

Hedin, Sven. 1903. *Central Asia and Tibet*. 2 vols. Hurst and Blackett, London.

Hedin, Sven. 1909. *Trans-Himalaya*. 2 vols. Macmillan and Co., London.

Prejevalsky [Przewalski], Nikolai. 1876. *Mongolia, the Tangut Country, and the solitudes of Northern Tibet*. 2 vols. Sampson Low, Marston, Searle, and Rivington, London.

Rawling, Cecil. 1905. *The great plateau*. Edward Arnold, London.

For those who cannot obtain the old expedition accounts, these two books provide informative summaries of the travels of explorers, adventurers, spies, pilgrims, and others, many of whom tried to reach the forbidden city of Lhasa:

Allen, Charles. 1982. *A mountain in Tibet*. André Deutsch, London.

Hopkirk, Peter. 1983. *Trespassers on the roof of the world*. J. P. Tarcher, Los Angeles.

This author entered Tibet in 1943 and lived in Lhasa from 1946 to 1950. The book describes the last days of old Tibet like no other:

Harrer, Heinrich. 1954. *Seven years in Tibet*. E. P. Dutton, New York.

The nomadic pastoralists have been largely ignored in the accounts of Tibet. The authors of this book lived with nomads in the Chang Tang. A balanced and insightful text and fine photographs chronicle the lives of these people:

Goldstein, Melvyn and **Cynthia Beall**. 1990. *Nomads of western Tibet, the survival of a way of life*. University of California Press, Berkeley.

When Tibet began to open to tourism in the 1980s, a new era in exploration began. Trekkers visited places few or no outsiders had ever seen. This author is an excellent guide to some of these sites:

McCue, Gary. 1991. *Trekking in Tibet, a traveler's guide*. The Mountaineers, Seattle.

Index